Especially for

....

From

....

Date

....

365
Encouraging
Prayers
for
Morning
& Evening

---·---

JOURNAL

---·---

BARBOUR
PUBLISHING

© 2016 by Barbour Publishing, Inc.

Compiled by Amy Oakley.

Print ISBN 978-1-63609-338-3

Devotional thoughts and prayers are from *Power Prayers for Your Life, Power Prayers to Grow Your Faith, Prayers and Promises for Times of Loss, 180 Prayers for a Woman of God*, and *Daily Conversations with God* published by Barbour Publishing, Inc.

Scripture quotations marked KJV are taken from the King James Version of the Bible.

Scripture quotations marked NKJV are taken from the New King James Version®. Copyright © 1982 by Thomas Nelson, Inc. Used by permission. All rights reserved.

Scripture quotations marked NIV are taken from the HOLY BIBLE, NEW INTERNATIONAL VERSION®. NIV®. Copyright © 1973, 1978, 1984, 2011 by Biblica, Inc.™ Used by permission. All rights reserved worldwide.

Scripture quotations marked MSG are from *THE MESSAGE*. Copyright © by Eugene H. Peterson 1993, 1994, 1995, 1996, 2000, 2001, 2002. Used by permission of NavPress Publishing Group.

Scripture quotations marked NLT are taken from the *Holy Bible*, New Living Translation copyright© 1996, 2004, 2007 by Tyndale House Foundation. Used by permission of Tyndale House Publishers, Inc. Carol Stream, Illinois 60188. All rights reserved.

Scripture quotations marked NCV are taken from the New Century Version of the Bible, copyright © 2005 by Thomas Nelson, Inc. Used by permission. All rights reserved.

Scripture quotations marked NASB are taken from the New American Standard Bible, © 1960, 1962, 1963, 1968, 1971, 1972, 1973, 1975, 1977, 1995 by The Lockman Foundation. Used by permission.

Scripture quotations marked AMP are taken from the Amplified® Bible, © 1954, 1958, 1962, 1964, 1965, 1987 by The Lockman Foundation. Used by permission.

Scripture quotations marked AMPC are taken from the Amplified® Bible, Classic Edition, Copyright © 1954, 1958, 1962, 1964, 1965, 1987 by The Lockman Foundation. Used by permission.

Scripture quotations marked CEV are from the Contemporary English Version, Copyright © 1995 by American Bible Society. Used by permission.

Published by Barbour Publishing, Inc., 1810 Barbour Drive, Uhrichsville, Ohio 44683, www.barbourbooks.com

Our mission is to inspire the world with the life-changing message of the Bible.

Member of the
Evangelical Christian
Publishers Association

Printed in China.

MORNING AND EVENING...

Encouragement for Your Soul

*Evening, and morning...will I pray,
and cry aloud: and he shall hear my voice.*

PSALM 55:17 KJV

365 Encouraging Prayers for Morning & Evening will help you experience
an intimate connection to the heavenly Father with a brief scripture and
prayer—twice a day for every day of the calendar year.

Enhance your spiritual journey with the peaceful time spent in prayer
and come to know just how deeply and tenderly God loves you.

Be blessed!

Morning
A FRESH START

Because of the LORD's great love we are not consumed, for his compassions never fail. They are new every morning; great is your faithfulness. I say to myself, "The LORD is my portion; therefore I will wait for him."
LAMENTATIONS 3:22–24 NIV

Heavenly Father, I come before You today and ask that You show me how to make You the focus of my day. Your love and compassion will never fail me, even when I fail You. I pray that You would remind of that every time I forget. Renew my spirit every morning, guide me in the path You have set before me, and keep my way straight. Amen.

....

....

....

....

Evening
GRACE FOR EVERYTHING

But he gives us more grace.
JAMES 4:6 NIV

Father, I'm thankful for Your grace—Your unmerited favor to me through Jesus Christ and that special strength You give Your child in times of need, trial, and temptation. Thank You for extending favor to me: forgiving my sins and adopting me into Your family. And thank You so much for that extra dose of perseverance that You keep giving to me in tough situations. I'm so thankful Your resource center will never experience a shortage. I praise You today for grace. Amen.

....

....

....

....

Morning

COME CLOSER, BELOVED

In him and through faith in him we may
approach God with freedom and confidence.
EPHESIANS 3:12 NIV

Dear Lord, You are the God of the universe, yet You ask me to come closer. You ask me to approach with freedom and confidence. I praise You for the great gift of Your Son, who allows me this access to You, my Creator. I am small, but I long to know You better. I am weak, but I know You have power to spare. Help me come to You again and again. In Jesus' precious name, amen.

....

....

....

....

Evening

FOR A MORE POSITIVE ATTITUDE

"For the LORD searches all hearts and
understands all the intent of the thoughts."
1 CHRONICLES 28:9 NKJV

Lord, You see the truth of how I think and feel. Help me let go of the things that have hurt me. I don't want that to be my focus. Let me focus on You and what You have planned for my life. Help me to do what I need to do without grumbling, complaining, or pointing fingers at others. Fill me with Your joy and strengthen me with Your love.

....

....

....

....

....

Morning
IN YOUR PRESENCE THIS DAY

"If my people, who are called by my name, will humble themselves and pray and seek my face and turn from their wicked ways, then I will hear from heaven."
2 CHRONICLES 7:14 NIV

Dear Father, I thank You that Your ear is always listening for the cries of Your people. You are always listening for my voice, and You know it out of billions of others. My words are not just spoken to the empty air, but You give them Your attention. Forgive me for my sins today, Lord, for they are many. I rest under Your mercy.

....

....

....

....

Evening
GUARDING MY MIND

You will keep in perfect peace those whose minds are steadfast, because they trust in you.
ISAIAH 26:3 NIV

Thank You for the helmet of salvation to protect my mind. As I spend time with You and in Your Word, I will become more like You. I will guard my mind and refuse to allow negative thoughts to have power over me. Your Word is my weapon to fight negative thoughts. I will be careful about the things I see and hear because I know they can affect my thinking. Help me to focus on truth.

....

....

....

....

Morning

EVERYTHING IS POSSIBLE

Abba, Father, all things are possible unto thee.
MARK 14:36 KJV

How amazing, Lord—my Father is the Creator of the universe! Your infinite creativity formed the beauty of the earth and the intricacies of life. I know I can rest assured in Your strength, in Your might, in Your abilities. There's nothing in heaven or on earth that You can't handle. Forgive me when I try to take things into my own hands. Since You made the world and everything in it, I know You can take care of my small life!

....

....

....

....

....

Evening

A TEACHABLE ATTITUDE

My son, pay attention to what I say; turn your ear to my words.
Do not let them out of your sight, keep them within your heart; for
they are life to those who find them and health to one's whole body.
PROVERBS 4:20–22 NIV

Holy Spirit, I invite You to be my teacher, to lead and guide me in all truth. Show me how to let go of selfish desires and listen to Your direction. I'll go where You want me to go today. Help me focus my energy on Your instruction.

....

....

....

....

Morning
RECEIVING JESUS

But as many as received him, to them gave he power to become
the sons of God, even to them that believe on his name.

JOHN 1:12 KJV

Lord, I believe in Your name. Help me every day to believe still more. Take away the doubts and insecurities that the world shouts at me every day. Keep my eyes firmly focused on You, even when troubles come. Keep my ears attuned to Your voice, especially when I am tempted to listen to other voices. I welcome You into my heart—to make a home there now and forever.

....

....

....

....

Evening
AN ATTITUDE OF MERCY

For the weapons of our warfare are not carnal but mighty in
God for pulling down strongholds, casting down arguments and
every high thing that exalts itself against the knowledge of God,
bringing every thought into captivity to the obedience of Christ.

2 CORINTHIANS 10:4–5 NKJV

Lord, when others treat me unfairly, judge me, or take something I feel I deserved, I want to get even. I want to fight for what is mine, but then I feel You urging me to show mercy. It's hard for me to do that.

....

....

....

....

....

Morning

THE ONE WHO IS

Who is like the LORD our God, who dwells on high?

PSALM 113:5 NKJV

Heavenly Father, today I'm grateful for all You are—the God who is, the God of the living, the great I AM. Your character is unchanging. You are the epitome of perfect holiness and love. Because of who and all You are, I believe and trust in You. Your truthfulness is indisputable and Your power is established. Not just for the majestic works by Your hand but for the pure glory of Your nature—I worship You today. Amen.

....

....

....

....

Evening

STRENGTH IN GOD

Praise the LORD! For he has heard my cry for mercy. The LORD is my strength and shield. I trust him with all my heart. He helps me, and my heart is filled with joy. I burst out in songs of thanksgiving.

PSALM 28:6–7 NLT

Lord, You are my strength and my shield. You give me courage to meet the challenges of the day. You build me up, leading me to places I would never have dreamed possible. You are the Friend who never leaves me, the Guide who walks before me. With You in my life, I can do anything.

....

....

....

....

....

Morning

NO WORRIES

*"I am leaving you with a gift—peace of mind and heart. And the peace
I give is a gift the world cannot give. So don't be troubled or afraid."*
JOHN 14:27 NLT

Lord, it's hard to find peace in this world. Help me avoid being distracted
by the noise. Once I come to You, within the stillness of these early morning
hours, my thoughts, heart, and spirit will be at rest. When I find You and
abide within You, I have no worries, no troubles, no fears. You are peace.
You are life.

....

....

....

....

Evening

THE LORD ALMIGHTY

*And [I] will be a Father unto you, and ye shall be
my sons and daughters, saith the Lord Almighty.*
2 CORINTHIANS 6:18 KJV

You, God, can do all things, for You are almighty and all-powerful. Because
You are my Father, I know I can trust You to handle each and every aspect
of my life. Show me new ways that I can rely on You to work in a mighty
way in my life. I trust You with my past, my present, and my future. You
are God, and I am not—and I am thankful that's the way it is.

....

....

....

....

....

Morning

ARISE AND GO

The word which came to Jeremiah from the LORD, saying: "Arise and go down to the potter's house, and there I will cause you to hear My words."

JEREMIAH 18:1–2 NKJV

So many times, Lord, I feel the urge to drop to my knees and pray, but I don't. I praise You that You keep calling my name again and again. Please help me trust You enough to stop what I am doing when I hear Your call. I am on my knees now, my King. I am listening to Your voice.

....

....

....

....

....

Evening

GOD'S WORD IS TRUTH

To the Jews who had believed him, Jesus said, "If you hold to my teaching, you are really my disciples. Then you will know the truth, and the truth will set you free."

JOHN 8:31–32 NIV

Thank You, Lord, that Your Word is true. I want to know the truth and live it. Help me look to Your steady and solid Word, not to this world, for my life instruction manual. I thank You that You will never lead me astray, that You never lie to me, and that You always keep Your promises.

....

....

....

....

....

Morning

A FATHER'S MERCY

I will be his father, and he shall be my son:
and I will not take my mercy away from him.

1 CHRONICLES 17:13 KJV

Thank You, Lord, for never taking Your mercy away from me. No matter how many times I let You down, I can always count on You to pick me back up. I cannot understand this gift, but I am thankful for it, Father. Please show me ways to extend mercy to others in my life—especially those whom the world may deem as "unlovable." Because the truth is, God, I know that most days I too am unlovable.

....

....

....

....

Evening

LIGHT FOR UNDERSTANDING

Your word is a lamp for my feet, a light on my path.

PSALM 119:105 NIV

Lord, Your Word is a lamp in my darkness—a flashlight on the path of life that helps me see the way. Your words enlighten me with wisdom, insight, and hope, even when I cannot see where I am going or how things will turn out. I'm so glad that You know the right direction. You have gone before me and are always with me, so I don't need to be afraid. I choose to follow Your leading.

....

....

....

....

....

Morning

GOD OF ALL COMFORT

Blessed be God. . .the Father of mercies, and the God of all comfort.

2 CORINTHIANS 1:3 KJV

You comfort me, Father, when my heart aches. When everything in my life seems to be going wrong. . .when the world is full of violence and disaster. . . when loss is everywhere I look. . .when hope is dying inside me, Your comfort never fails. Thank You for offering me that constant care in my life. Help me to always extend comfort, care, and compassion to others as well—ultimately leading them to You.

....

....

....

....

....

Evening

GOD'S WORD IS POWERFUL

For the word of God is alive and active. Sharper than any double-
edged sword, it penetrates even to dividing soul and spirit, joints
and marrow; it judges the thoughts and attitudes of the heart.

HEBREWS 4:12 NIV

I can't hide from You, Lord, for You already know everything. With Your conviction comes repentance and forgiveness. You accept me as I am and give me the grace and power to make lasting changes in my life. The Word of God is living and active. That's why it has so much power. I give You my thoughts and attitudes and ask for healing.

....

....

....

....

Morning

I WILL HEAR

"Before they call I will answer; while they are still speaking I will hear."
ISAIAH 65:24 NIV

Dear Lord, I praise You for being the God who hears. I praise You that You know my heart even before *I* do. I rest in the fact that You are answering my prayer, even before I pray. Help me be more like You, Lord. So often I don't take time to listen with love to the people around me. I need Your ears and Your heart, Lord. Speak to me and through me. Amen.

....

....

....

....

....

Evening

EQUIPPED FOR GOOD WORK

All Scripture is God-breathed and is useful for teaching, rebuking,
correcting and training in righteousness, so that the servant of
God may be thoroughly equipped for every good work.
2 TIMOTHY 3:16–17 NIV

Lord, Your Word tells me that You breathed Your life into the words that men put on parchment—which are now the words of the Bible I read. Teach me, Lord. Correct and train me in righteousness so that I will be ready for whatever life holds for me today.

....

....

....

....

....

Morning
A GODLY CONFIDENCE

Now this is the confidence that we have in Him, that if
we ask anything according to His will, He hears us.

1 JOHN 5:14 NKJV

Dear Lord, sometimes I feel like my prayers are just a long list of wishes, as though You're some sort of celestial genie. I'm so thankful You are not. You don't give me what I want just because I want it. I thank You that You give me only what is in line with Your will for me. So, Lord, show me what that is. Reveal Your will, and show me how and for what You want me to pray.

....

....

....

....

Evening
WISDOM IN INTERPRETATION

Do your best to present yourself to God as one approved, a worker who
does not need to be ashamed and who correctly handles the word of truth.

2 TIMOTHY 2:15 NIV

Lord, teach me to read Your word, meditate on it, and apply it to my life. Give me a hunger for spending time with You—and wisdom when I teach Your Word to others. I want to be a person who correctly handles the Word of Truth. Enlighten me and give me understanding that I may live right and bring glory to Your name.

....

....

....

....

....

Morning
WHAT MANNER OF LOVE

Behold, what manner of love the Father hath bestowed
upon us, that we should be called the sons of God.
1 JOHN 3:1 KJV

A good father protects his children; he loves his children unconditionally; he understands and forgives his children; he provides for his family; he is intimately involved in the lives of those he loves. You are more than a good father, God—You are the *perfect* Father. Remind me, Lord, that *this* is the way You love me. Thank You for loving all of me—unconditionally and without reservation.

....
....
....
....

Evening
TO KNOW GOD'S WILL

For this reason, since the day we heard about you, we have not stopped
praying for you. We continually ask God to fill you with the knowledge of
his will through all the wisdom and understanding that the Spirit gives.
COLOSSIANS 1:9 NIV

Lord, I want to know Your will for my life. Enlighten me with wisdom, discernment, and understanding. Show me when to stay and when to go, when to speak and when to close my mouth. Fill me with the knowledge of Your best for me—right now and in the future. Help me obediently and joyfully accept Your answers.

....
....
....
....

Morning
LIGHTS

That ye may be blameless and harmless, the sons of God,
without rebuke, in the midst of a crooked and perverse
nation, among whom ye shine as lights in the world.
PHILIPPIANS 2:15 KJV

Lord, I am grateful that I can claim You as my Father. Because You live in my heart, I am Your representative to the world around me. Thank You for using me for Your purpose, and thank You for filling in the gaps where I am inadequate to do Your work. Make me Your light in the world around me, not so I can gain fame for myself but only to proclaim Your awesomeness.

Evening
REVIVE ME!

The law of the LORD is perfect, reviving the soul. The statutes
of the LORD are trustworthy, making wise the simple.
PSALM 19:7 NIV

Lord, sometimes life gets so crazy. I get so tired and stressed out from working hard at my job—whether it's in the home or in the marketplace. I long to bask in Your presence and find refreshment. Revive my soul with Your Word. Immerse me in Your life-giving truth, and turn the dark places in my life to light so I can radiate Jesus in my corner of the world.

Morning
GOOD GIFTS

*"If you, despite being evil, know how to give good gifts to
your children, how much more will your Father who is
in heaven give good things to those who ask Him!"*
MATTHEW 7:11 NASB

Lord, You are a loving, generous God, slow to anger and rich in love. I pray that the riches You offer through Christ will be visible in my life, so that others will be drawn to You. I have nothing to offer them except You, Jesus. You have so much, and You long to open the storehouses of heaven to us, blessings pressed down and running over. Amen.

....

....

....

....

Evening
GIVE ME JOY

*The precepts of the LORD are right, giving joy to the heart.
The commands of the LORD are radiant, giving light to the eyes.*
PSALM 19:8 NIV

Lord, Your words are right and true; they bring joy to my heart. I need more joy in my life. Happiness comes and goes, but joy is deep and lasting. I need Your true joy despite my circumstances and my feelings. Your commands illuminate me so I can sing Your praises and live revitalized each day. Thank You for Your joy, Lord.

....

....

....

....

....

Morning

CHILDREN OF THE RESURRECTION

*Neither can they die any more: for they are. . .the children
of God, being the children of the resurrection.*

LUKE 20:36 KJV

Because I am Your child, I don't need to be afraid of death. You Yourself conquered death and the grave on Easter morning, and You promise me that Your grace will save me from eternal death as well. How amazing and wonderful and humbling! I am so glad, Lord, for the promise of Your resurrection and the assurance of eternity with You in heaven. Help me be bold in sharing this wonderful hope with people who have no hope.

....

....

....

....

Evening

INTEGRITY OF THE WORD

*Keep this Book of the Law always on your lips; meditate on
it day and night, so that you may be careful to do everything
written in it. Then you will be prosperous and successful.*

JOSHUA 1:8 NIV

Father, I have great respect for Your Word. I give it first place in my life. Your Word is my umpire, settling disputes and answering questions that I face every day. I refuse to compromise. I set my heart upon the foundation of Your Word and will not be moved from it.

....

....

....

....

....

Morning

ALCHEMY FOR A RAINY DAY

My voice shalt thou hear in the morning, O LORD; in the morning will I direct my prayer unto thee, and will look up.

PSALM 5:3 KJV

Dear Lord, it's so dark this morning. I don't want to be here in this gray light. I just want to be where You are. I want to be with You, walking on streets of gold, with the light of Your glory shining on my face. I long for that endless golden day. Please come to me, Lord, and shine Your love and light on my heart this morning. Amen.

....

....

....

....

....

Evening

PEACE

Grace unto you, and peace, from God our Father.

2 THESSALONIANS 1:2 KJV

Thank You, Father, for the gift of Your peace. Help me remember that Your peace is the only true and lasting rest for my soul—and to always run to You instead of an idol in my life. When troubles come my way, please give me an extra dose of Your peace. And when I see others in turmoil, help me always be ready with a word and an action that will help them seek out Your peace.

....

....

....

....

Morning

WAITING ON GOD

I long, yes, I faint with longing to enter the courts of the LORD. With my whole being, body and soul, I will shout joyfully to the living God.

PSALM 84:2 NLT

My feet are positioned at the starting line. I'm ready to run the race. All I need now is Your signal for me to begin it. I believe I've found my passion and I'm ready to act on it, but I know I need to wait for Your timing. Help me be patient. Alert me to what I still need to do in making my preparations.

....

....

....

....

....

Evening

OUR REAL CALLING

That you would walk worthy of God who calls you into His own kingdom and glory.

1 THESSALONIANS 2:12 NKJV

Dear Lord, this is my true calling: walking worthily into Your kingdom and glory. My calling as a teacher is but a reflection of Your highest priority. May I order my steps in such a way as to be worthy of Your calling, spiritually and professionally. Help me, Father, to show Your life within me to the world outside. May it be clear to those around me that You are the Lord of my life.

....

....

....

....

....

Morning

TWENTY-FOUR

This is the day which the LORD hath made; we will rejoice and be glad in it.
PSALM 118:24 KJV

I thank You for this day, Lord, with its twenty-four precious hours. Only twenty-four. That never seems like enough, yet I'm always glad to fall into bed when they're over. How many of those hours do I give to You, Lord? Not even *one*, maybe two on Sundays? Thank You for continuing to remind me that relationships require *time*, and I vow to give You more of each day—each day that is already a gift from You. Amen.

....

....

....

....

....

Evening

STANDING UP FOR MY FAITH

Let the message about Christ, in all its richness, fill your lives. Teach and counsel each other with all the wisdom he gives. Sing psalms and hymns and spiritual songs to God with thankful hearts.
COLOSSIANS 3:16 NLT

Heavenly Father, I want to let my light shine before all people. Teach me to act in a way that speaks Your truth to others. Fill me with an undying passion to see lives changed for Your glory. When I'm called to defend my faith, help me do it in love, with gentleness and respect.

....

....

....

....

Morning
WHAT PLEASES GOD

*How much more shall the blood of Christ, who through the
eternal Spirit offered Himself without spot to God, cleanse
your conscience from dead works to serve the living God?*

HEBREWS 9:14 NKJV

God, I want to be passionate about the purpose You have for me. Show me
the things in my life that please You, and give me the courage and strength
to pursue those things. Keep my purpose before me, fill my heart, and give
me right motives to accomplish all You have set before me. As long as You
are with me and my focus is on what pleases You, I cannot fail.

....

....

....

....

Evening
FALLING

*Cast your cares on the LORD and he will sustain you;
he will never let the righteous be shaken.*

PSALM 55:22 NIV

Dear Father, today I said some things I regret. I hurt people I care about,
and worse, I hurt You, Lord. I am so sorry. Please forgive me and redeem
my angry, selfish words. I am so glad that You tell us in Your Word to
forgive seventy times seven times, because I know that is how many times
You will forgive me. Thanks be to Jesus that when I fall, I am falling into
Your arms. Amen.

....

....

....

....

Morning
SPIRIT-LED

For as many as are led by the Spirit of God, they are the sons of God.
ROMANS 8:14 KJV

Father, let Your Spirit lead me in each thing. Let me always look to You for guidance and direction. Keep me away from the temptation of following the paths of other "gods." Make Your Spirit alive and active in my heart, so that I might hear Your voice every day, in my every decision, and in my every action. Forgive me when I ignore the movement of Your Spirit. Make Him active in my heart, Lord!

....

....

....

....

....

Evening
A WORTHY LIFE

As a prisoner for the Lord, then, I urge you to live
a life worthy of the calling you have received.
EPHESIANS 4:1 NIV

Lord Jesus, I'm not locked up in jail as the apostle Paul often was, but I'm enslaved by love to You. You have called me to faith—and to my vocation. I take them both seriously and want to live a life worthy of these callings. I thank You, Lord, that You empower me to do both.

....

....

....

....

....

Morning
PRAISE!

"For then you will take pleasure in the Almighty and lift up your face to God."
Job 22:26 NASB

Dear Father, today I just want to praise You! You are merciful, You are awesome, You are holy! You are beyond compare. You are my Maker and Sustainer. You saved me! You are Light and Love and all that is good. Lord, You made *mountains*. And trees that spear the clouds and birds as bright as rainbows and flowers as small and perfect as a baby's fingernail. Who is like You? Amen and amen and amen.

....

....

....

....

Evening
A HOPEFUL VISION

Where there is no revelation, the people cast off restraint; but happy is he who keeps the law.
Proverbs 29:18 NKJV

Lord, we would surely perish if we didn't have the vision of Your plan for our lives. You supply us for our duties each day, and You will accomplish Your desire through us wherever we work. I can trust You in the good times—when the job is going smoothly—as well as those times when Your design is less clear. Give me a vision, Lord—of You and of what You're accomplishing through me.

....

....

....

....

....

Morning

THE DAY OF SMALL THINGS

For who hath despised the day of small things? for they shall rejoice.
ZECHARIAH 4:10 KJV

Dear Lord, I ask for thankfulness in the small things. I yearn to see each day as a gift—swathed in sunrise—to be unwrapped. Thank You for moments that remind me that ordinary days are really shot through with holiness. I thank You now, Lord, for those gifts and the gifts that I will see *You've already given me* as I learn to live in thankfulness. Amen.

....

....

....

....

....

Evening

CALLED ACCORDING TO HIS PURPOSE

*Who saved us and called us with a holy calling, not according
to our works, but according to His own purpose and grace,
which was granted to us in Christ Jesus from all eternity.*
2 TIMOTHY 1:9 NASB

Dear God, I thank You that our calling is dependent not upon our own efforts but upon Your purpose and the grace You gave us in Jesus. Your purpose is never random but something You've planned for all time. I want to be one with You in Your eternal purpose of bringing people to know You.

....

....

....

....

....

Morning

EXPECTING MIRACLES

Then the fire of the LORD fell and consumed the burnt sacrifice, and the wood and the stones and the dust, and it licked up the water that was in the trench.

1 KINGS 18:38 NKJV

Dear God, I come before You today, knowing You are a God who works miracles. You heal the blind, the lame, the leprous, the demon possessed. You crack open prison cells, turn night into day, and roll the ocean up like a scroll. You send down fire from heaven. You bring the dead back to life. Please answer my prayer today. Work my small miracle. Amen.

....

....

....

....

Evening

SHARING MY CHALLENGES

Be an example to the believers with your words, your actions, your love, your faith, and your pure life.

1 TIMOTHY 4:12 NCV

Father, You know all of my hurts and pains. I know I went through those difficulties for a reason, perhaps to encourage others. Help me be quick to share with anyone who might benefit from what I have endured. Help me share how I learned to trust in You through each challenge. Give me the words to encourage them to hold tightly to You during their hardships.

....

....

....

....

....

Morning
LIVING WORDS

O Lord, You are my God. I will exalt You, I will praise Your name, for You have done wonderful things; Your counsels of old are faithfulness and truth.
ISAIAH 25:1 NKJV

Dear God, Your Word is thousands of years old and tells stories even older. How many books made millennia ago are still useful today? Lord, I can't think of even one. Your Word is as true today as when the ink was wet. It is beautiful. It is inspiring. It is rich. It surprises. It sustains. It transforms. I praise the living Word.

Evening
TO LIVE WHAT I BELIEVE

Walk by the Spirit, and you will not carry out the desire of the flesh.
GALATIANS 5:16 NASB

Lord, forgive me when my choices don't line up with what I believe. Help me nurture Your Word in my heart so I grow to maturity. Teach me Your ways, and give me understanding of Your instructions. Allow the values of my faith to affect every area of my life. Convict me when I am tempted to stray from truth. Help me stay committed as I grow in faith and in my relationship with You.

Morning
PEACEMAKERS

Blessed are the peacemakers: for they shall be called the children of God.
MATTHEW 5:9 KJV

Dear Lord, teach me that if I want the world to see me as Your child, then I need to always work for peace in the world around me. Help me resist the temptation to stir up bitterness or anger among my family, friends, and neighbors. Take away angry words that may well up in the heat of the moment. Instead, teach me to be a peacemaker—so that others can't help but acknowledge that You are living and active within me.

....

....

....

....

....

Evening
CREATED FOR GOOD WORKS

We are God's masterpiece. He has created us anew in Christ Jesus,
so we can do the good things he planned for us long ago.
EPHESIANS 2:10 NLT

You have shaped me into the unique person I am today. You have created me to do good works. I am awed that You prepared things in advance for me to do. From the very beginning, You made me for a specific job in Your kingdom. Give me the courage to take hold of that task. Help me resist shying away from the challenges that face me.

....

....

....

....

Morning

THE WATCHER

The LORD will keep you from all harm—he will watch over your life; the LORD will watch over your coming and going both now and forevermore.
PSALM 121:7–8 NIV

Lord, I'm scared. I'm scared of someone I love getting sick. I'm scared of being abandoned. I'm scared of hurting the ones I love. I'm scared that I'll grow old and die before You return. But mostly I'm scared of never knowing You better than I know You right now. Thank You for that fear, Lord, and how it drives me to my knees again and again. Amen.

....

....

....

....

....

Evening

SERVING FROM THE HEART

As slaves of Christ, do the will of God with all your heart.
EPHESIANS 6:6 NLT

I want to work for You, Lord, using all my heart, soul, and talent. I want to be Your tool, serving You with passion. And as I do so, help me keep my eyes and focus on You rather than the gift You have given me. Help me understand what You have shaped me to do.

....

....

....

....

....

....

Morning
LOVING OUR ENEMIES

But love ye your enemies, and do good, and lend, hoping for nothing again;
and your reward shall be great, and ye shall be the children of the Highest.
LUKE 6:35 KJV

Heavenly Father, I have a hard time loving some of the people in my life.
Your Word says that You want me to repay evil for good. Remind me that
You ask me to not only love my enemies but to also do them positive,
active good, without thought of reward. It's not going to be easy, Lord,
but with Your help, I can do it.

....

....

....

....

Evening
GENUINE AUTHENTICITY

"These people show honor to me with words, but their hearts are far from me."
MATTHEW 15:8 NCV

Lord, help me be a true reflection of Your heart in all that I do. Remind
me that my actions should not be for attention, praise, or position. I want
my motives to always be pure. Help me discern my real intentions when I
decide to do something. Keep me honest and remind me that I represent
You in the choices I make. In everything I pursue, help me above all to be
committed to my relationship with You.

....

....

....

....

....

Morning

THE DEAD WILL LIVE!

But your dead will live, LORD; their bodies will rise—
let those who dwell in the dust wake up and shout for joy.

ISAIAH 26:19 NIV

Dear Lord, I feel so sad this morning. I miss certain people so badly. They are all dead, Lord, and that seems so strange and wrong. They are in the ground, out of reach. Thank You for comforting me with the assurance that it is wrong, that death was not part of Your plan. And that, ultimately, it will be swallowed up in victory. My loved ones will wake up and shout for joy. Hallelujah!

....

....

....

....

....

Evening

FORGIVE EACH OTHER

Get rid of all bitterness, rage and anger, brawling
and slander, along with every form of malice.

EPHESIANS 4:31 NIV

Lord, forgiveness can sometimes be so hard. I need Your help to get rid of bitterness and anger. Help me build others up instead of putting them down—even when it seems they deserve the latter. Teach us grace. Help us forgive one another and be kind and compassionate, because we know Christ forgave all of us.

....

....

....

....

Morning

CONSTANT PRAISE

Rejoice always, pray without ceasing.

1 THESSALONIANS 5:16–17 NASB

Lord, You gave me life, and I praise You. You filled my lungs with air from my very first breath, and I praise You. I praise You because I am fearfully and wonderfully made. Today, Lord, I want to pray to You like I breathe: in and out, all day long. Fill my mouth with Your praise. Let my lips be always whispering Your name. Let my heart beat to the rhythm of Your perfect will. Amen.

Evening

OBEDIENCE LEADS TO JOY

"If you keep my commands, you will remain in my love, just as I have kept my Father's commands and remain in his love."

JOHN 15:10 NIV

Lord, Your Word says that if we obey Your commands, we will remain in Your love. I want to serve You out of an obedient heart. Just as Jesus submits to You, Father, I choose to submit to You too. Obedience leads to a blessing. Empower me, encourage me, and give me the will to want to make decisions that lead to a better life and greater joy.

Morning

RECORD OF WRONGS

[Love] does not demand its own way. It is not
irritable, and it keeps no record of being wronged.
1 CORINTHIANS 13:5 NLT

I can't seem to help myself, Lord. I have this list in my mind of all the things people have done to hurt me. I cannot seem to let them go. Help me give up on this record of wrongs. Give me a clean slate this morning and every morning. Help me resist bringing up the past and have hope for tomorrow. May the power of love erase all these wrongs and give me peace.

....

....

....

....

....

Evening

GOD'S OFFSPRING

For in him we live, and move, and have our
being. . . For we are also his offspring.
ACTS 17:28 KJV

The world tells me to be independent, self-sufficient, and to stand on my own two feet. But the truth is that I am intimately connected to the Lord of the universe, and I rely on You for my life, Father. Most days it's a relief that it's not all on me to handle everything. To put it another way, You and I are kinfolk, Lord! I would not exist if it were not for You.

....

....

....

....

Morning
CALL TO ME

*"Call to me and I will answer you and tell you great
and unsearchable things you do not know."*
JEREMIAH 33:3 NIV

O Lord of the universe, You know everything; You see everything; You are everywhere; You are every*time* and eternal. Lord, sometimes we think that we are so smart, we people that You *made*. Compared to You, we are babies one minute old, looking up at the light and blinking, unable to comprehend anything. But You want us to grow up, Lord. You long to teach us everything You know. I yield my heart and mind to You. Amen.

....

....

....

....

Evening
WHO KNOWS?

*Beloved, now are we the sons of God,
and it doth not yet appear what we shall be.*
1 JOHN 3:2 KJV

Father, I'm grateful for being Your child in this life. I can't even imagine what that will mean in the life to come! Thank You for the hope You have given to me, for now and for an unknown future. Although I don't know all the details of what You have in store, I am thankful I can rest secure, knowing You have it all under control.

....

....

....

....

....

Morning

LIVING DAILY WITH DELIGHT

You will go out in joy and be led forth in peace.
ISAIAH 55:12 NIV

Lord, thank You for the joy You bring every day. Joy is with me—because You are there. Lead me forth today in peace. May all of creation—even the trees of the field—praise You as I praise You. Help me live with a lighter heart and a positive attitude, despite the distractions and duties that seek to steal my joy. I choose You. Help me live daily with Your delight.

....
....
....
....
....
....

Evening

FINDING JOY IN GOD'S PRESENCE

The LORD has done great things for us, and we are filled with joy.
PSALM 126:3 NIV

Lord, draw me closer to You. In Your presence is fullness of joy—and I want to be filled. Knowing I am loved by You makes me glad; I cannot imagine life without You. With You there is light; without You, darkness. With You there is pleasure; without You, pain. You care; You comfort; You really listen. Here, in Your presence, I am loved, I am renewed, and I am very happy.

....
....
....
....
....

Morning

THE JOY OF KNOWING JESUS

But let all who take refuge in you be glad; let them ever sing for joy. Spread your protection over them, that those who love your name may rejoice in you.

PSALM 5:11 NIV

Jesus, knowing You brings me joy! Thank You for the abundant life You provide. I can smile because I know that You love me. I can be positive because You have the power to heal, restore, and revive. Your presence brings me joy—being with You is such a privilege. I delight to know You and tell others about You.

....

....

....

....

....

Evening

MAKE ME WISER

If any of you lacks wisdom, let him ask of God, who gives to all liberally and without reproach, and it will be given to him.

JAMES 1:5 NKJV

Dear Father, today I stumbled up against something that calls for Your wisdom. I want to be used by You in people's lives, but first I need Your wisdom. I'm no Solomon, Lord, but just like he did, I'm asking for Your wisdom. Thank You that You promise to give it to me freely and generously. Amen.

....

....

....

....

....

Morning

THE CONFIDENCE OF FIRSTHAND KNOWLEDGE

I've got my eye on the goal, where God is beckoning us onward—
to Jesus. I'm off and running, and I'm not turning back.

PHILIPPIANS 3:14 MSG

Lord, it all comes down to knowing You. I don't ask for supernatural revelation, Lord. I just ask for a dogged determination to know You better, verse by verse. I ask for a continual filling of Your Spirit so that my eyes and heart are wide open to You. Then I can say *amen* with confidence. And I will: Amen!

....

....

....

....

Evening

A THANKFUL HEART

Rejoice always, pray continually, give thanks in all
circumstances; for this is God's will for you in Christ Jesus.

1 THESSALONIANS 5:16–18 NIV

Lord, You are my God—and it is my joy to give You my inner heart. Cleanse me, fill me, heal me, and help me live with a joyful, thankful heart. I want to be a woman of prayer. I want to make a difference in my world. For all You are and all You do, I am grateful. I give You praise for the blessings in my life.

....

....

....

....

....

Morning

GOD IS LOVE

God is love; and he that dwelleth in love dwelleth in God, and God in him.

1 JOHN 4:16 KJV

God, let me never forget that You are love—patient, kind, not envious, not proud, not rude, not self-seeking, not easily angered, keeping no record of wrong. You do not delight in evil, but You rejoice in the truth. You always protect, trust, hope, and persevere. Your love will always remain. It is the greatest thing there is. May I always make my home within You—within Your love.

....

....

....

....

Evening

YOU DON'T HAVE TO BE PERFECT

For the law was given through Moses;
grace and truth came through Jesus Christ.

JOHN 1:17 NIV

Lord, when I struggle with perfectionism, help me break this bondage. I know it's a good thing to want things to be right, but it can go too far. I want to live in Your grace, not under the "law" that keeps me under this burden. Heal me from judging myself and my actions too harshly—and fearing the judgment of others. Help me see, Lord, that because of Your mercy and grace, I am good enough.

....

....

....

....

....

Morning

THE SALVATION OF EVERYONE!

For I am not ashamed of the gospel of Christ: for it is the
power of God unto salvation to every one that believeth.

ROMANS 1:16 KJV

Dear God, I am not patient about waiting for the things I long for with all
my heart. But You are patient, Lord. You are waiting. You are waiting for
us. You won't return until everyone has had a chance to hear the Gospel.
Your incredible patience and love is greater than our persistent sin. Who
can I tell, Lord? Who is near me who hasn't yet heard or understood the
Good News?

....

....

....

....

Evening

DEALING WITH PRIDE

Do not think of yourself more highly than you ought, but
rather think of yourself with sober judgment, in accordance
with the faith God has distributed to each of you.

ROMANS 12:3 NIV

Lord, help me avoid pride, arrogance, and conceit in my heart—but when I
give in, please forgive me. Humble me, Lord, and lift me up to be a willing
servant. With my eyes on You, not on myself, may I see the needs in the
lives of others.

....

....

....

....

....

Morning
WISDOM AND MIGHT

Blessed be the name of God for ever and ever: for wisdom and might are his.
DANIEL 2:20 KJV

Lord, You are wise. I will never fully grasp the vastness of Your wisdom, but I am thankful to have that strength in my corner. Scripture says that along with being all-wise, You're all-powerful as well. The heavens and the earth are at Your beck and call. No matter how powerful we humans think we are, You are the One who holds it all. Today I am relying on Your wisdom and might.

....

....

....

....

Evening
THE VALUE OF REST

Do you not know? Have you not heard? The LORD is the everlasting God, the Creator of the ends of the earth. He will not grow tired or weary, and his understanding no one can fathom.
ISAIAH 40:28 NIV

Lord, I come to You for respite. Like a rest in music breaks the tension, I need a break too. May I find healing and strength in quietness and solitude. Give me the courage to be still, to cease striving, and to be with You. Replenish me in Your presence, Lord.

....

....

....

....

....

Morning

THE CHEERLEADER

I can do all things through Christ who strengthens me.
PHILIPPIANS 4:13 NKJV

Dear Lord, in this verse I can hear You cheering me on. What can I do? *All things!* Who's going to help me? *Christ!* What's He going to do? *Strengthen me!* I praise You for bringing these particular words to me right now. Your Word is so amazing: written thousands of years ago, yet it speaks to us perfectly in our moment of need. I know I am going to need this verse today, Lord. Help me sing it back to You all day long. Amen.

....

....

....

....

....

Evening

CONFIDENCE

The LORD will be at your side and will keep your foot from being snared.
PROVERBS 3:26 NIV

Lord, help me have more confidence—not in myself but in You. I don't want to be proud or conceited, but I don't want to be a doormat either. Give me a teachable heart. You have so much to show me, and I want to learn Your ways. Learning and growing, I am alive! I am totally dependent on You, Lord. Full of Your Spirit, I can stand confident and strong.

....

....

....

....

....

Morning
THE GOD OF HOSTS

For, lo, he that formeth the mountains, and createth the wind,
and declareth unto man what is his thought, that maketh
the morning darkness, and treadeth upon the high places
of the earth, The Lord, The God of hosts, is his name.

AMOS 4:13 KJV

God, my Father, You formed the mountains and the wind, the dark of nighttime and the morning's light, and You lead all the hosts of heaven. You formed my intricate features inside my mother's womb. Let me never take for granted Your limitless creativity. Let me never forget who You truly are.

....

....

....

....

....

Evening
A PERSON OF WISDOM

Blessed are those who find wisdom, those who gain understanding,
for she is more profitable than silver and yields better returns than gold.

PROVERBS 3:13–14 NIV

Lord, I want to be a person of wisdom, not foolishness. Help me make right choices and conduct myself in a manner worthy of Your name. I pray that I would be honest and upright in my daily life so my actions reflect who You are. Help me act with integrity, keeping promises and commitments.

....

....

....

....

Morning

THE CONSTRUCTION SITE

*Being confident of this, that he who began a good work in you
will carry it on to completion until the day of Christ Jesus.*

PHILIPPIANS 1:6 NIV

God, I am a work in progress. Sometimes I feel like there should be a barrier
of construction tape up around my rough edges. I am not who I want to be
yet, Lord, and I know I'm not who *You* want me to be. You love me anyway.
Thank You for Your mercy and the sure promise that You *are* carrying out
Your work in me. Give me fertile soil and a yielding heart. Amen.

....

....

....

....

....

Evening

LIVING A LIFE OF LOVE

"Love your neighbor as yourself."

MATTHEW 22:39 NIV

Lord, I want to live a life of love! Show me what true love is—Your love—so
I can receive it and give it away to others. Teach me to care for my neighbor
as I would care for myself. Let love be my motivation for action. Help me
speak kind, encouraging words and bless others with my actions as well. I
thank You that Your amazing, unconditional, accepting love sustains me.

....

....

....

....

....

Morning
WORRY LINES

Instead of worrying, pray. Let petitions and praises shape
your worries into prayers, letting God know your concerns.
PHILIPPIANS 4:6 MSG

Dear Lord, I praise You for how You are changing me. I praise You for how You are teaching me to lift my worries up to You. I trust You. Lord, the only worry lines I want are the creases in the pages of my Bible. *You* are the overcomer; *You* are my resting place; *You* are my strength and my fortress. I am so relieved to lay my worries before You and let them become prayers. Amen.

....

....

....

....

Evening
MAKING PRAYER A PRIORITY

Blessed is the man that trusteth in the LORD, and whose hope the LORD is.
JEREMIAH 17:7 KJV

Lord, I feel like a withered plant with dry, brown leaves. Help me connect with You in prayer so I can grow strong and healthy, inside and out, like a vibrant green tree. You are my source of living water. Teach me to be still, to listen, to absorb what You want to reveal to me. In this holy conversation, may I find freedom, peace, and joy—and a closer walk with You.

....

....

....

....

....

Morning
IF I CAN

Jesus said, "If? There are no 'ifs' among believers. Anything can happen."
MARK 9:23 MSG

God, You are so amazing! When You first saved me, I suddenly felt like the world had shifted under me, and anything was possible. Even simple things were made new. The knowledge that You did miracles (and might for me too) made me feel like I was standing on the edge of a new kind of life that was so beautiful and grand I might explode with joy. It's not just a feeling, Lord. Anything *can* happen. I praise You with open wonder. Amen.

....

....

....

....

....

Evening
A MATTER OF SIGNIFICANCE

To them God willed to make known what are the riches of the glory of this mystery among the Gentiles: which is Christ in you, the hope of glory.
COLOSSIANS 1:27 NKJV

Jesus, help me find my identity in You. I know that my relationship with You is significant. As I read the Bible, give me an understanding of who You created me to be. Point out the true identity that has been given to me through the gift of salvation and my relationship with You.

....

....

....

....

....

Morning
MAGNIFYING GLASSES

O magnify the LORD with me, and let us exalt his name together.
PSALM 34:3 KJV

Remind me, Father God, that I am called to be Your magnifying glass. Shine Your light through me to all the world around me. Move me out of the way so that it's all You that others see. My aim is to exalt Your name in everything I do—in thought, word, and deed. Lead me to other people who are like minded so that we can truly live lives that worship You and only You.

....

....

....

....

....

Evening
I AM GOD'S CHILD

The Spirit of God, who raised Jesus from the dead, lives in you.
ROMANS 8:11 NLT

Jesus, thank You for providing the way for me to belong to Your family. I am born of God—not from natural birth but spiritual birth. You are my example, and I will do my best to follow in Your footsteps. I want to be like You and our heavenly Father. I want to have the same character and nature. I receive Your gift of inclusion in the greatest family of all eternity.

....

....

....

....

....

....

Morning
OUR REDEEMER

As for our redeemer, the LORD of hosts is his name, the Holy One of Israel.
ISAIAH 47:4 KJV

You are my Redeemer, Lord—You have saved me from all that separated me from You. When I am not holy, You are. When I am trapped in anxiety and despair, You free me. When I see no hope of escape from my present circumstance, You rescue me. When I feel unworthy and stained beyond all hope of saving, You cover me with grace. I worship Your name, Your presence, Your beauty, and Your strength.

....

....

....

....

....

Evening
GOD BLESS THIS HOUSE

The LORD's curse is on the house of the wicked,
but he blesses the home of the righteous.
PROVERBS 3:33 NIV

Lord, please bless this house. We ask that You would bring protection and safety to this place. Fill each room with Your loving presence, Your peace, and Your power. May we treat one another with respect, with warmth and welcome for others. Use this house to bring glory to Your name, Lord. May all who come here feel at home.

....

....

....

....

Morning
BABY BLUE

He tends his flock like a shepherd: he gathers the lambs in his arms and carries them close to his heart; he gently leads those that have young.
ISAIAH 40:11 NIV

Lord, I lift up to You a new mother who is struggling with postpartum depression. Help her hold on while she heals and adjusts. Surround her with people who will love and support her in practical ways. Be with her husband and little one too. Lord, use this time so that they will look back on it and marvel at how You drew them closer to each other and to You. Amen.

....

....

....

....

....

Evening
THE POWER OF RECOGNIZING SEASONS

To everything there is a season, a time for every purpose under heaven.
ECCLESIASTES 3:1 NKJV

Father, I know there is a season for everything. The Bible tells me there is a time for every purpose under heaven—a time to weep, a time to laugh, a time to mourn, and a time to dance. Help me recognize the season I am in, and help me flow with it. I don't want to be resistant. Show me how to bend with Your leading.

....

....

....

....

....

Morning

THE GOD OF OUR SALVATION

Help us, O God of our salvation, for the glory of thy name:
and deliver us, and purge away our sins, for thy name's sake.

PSALM 79:9 KJV

When I start to look to other things for my salvation—money, prestige, people, things—remind me, God, that You are the only One who can save me now and keep me safe forever. Remove the temptations from my life that I am so quick to turn to when I'm stressed and insecure. Make me aware of the pitfalls that surround me. Focus my attention on You and Your kingdom.

....

....

....

....

Evening

ENCOURAGING WORDS

Gracious words are a honeycomb, sweet to the soul and healing to the bones.

PROVERBS 16:24 NIV

Lord, I pray that we would speak encouraging and kind words in our home. Help us to build one another up—never to tear one another down. Help us avoid being so self-absorbed that we forget to ask how others around us are doing. Like honey, may the words from our mouths be sweet to the soul and healing to the bones. Help us be positive, peaceable, and considerate. Thank You for giving us words that restore.

....

....

....

....

....

Morning

WHO ARE YOUR PHILISTINES?

"The LORD will cause your enemies who rise against you to be defeated before your face; they shall come out against you one way and flee before you seven ways."
DEUTERONOMY 28:7 NKJV

I am not a warrior, Lord, but I do have enemies. Enemies of anger, self-control, discontent, pride, selfishness, laziness. Strengthen me today for my battles against these foes. You are my high commander, Lord. Strengthen me with Your Spirit so I will be able to resist the enemy of my soul and follow only You. Amen.

....

....

....

....

Evening

PLANNING AHEAD

The ants are not a strong people, but they prepare their food in the summer.
PROVERBS 30:25 NASB

Lord, my life gets so busy that I seem to get stuck in the moment. Remind me to lift up my head and look to the future. Help me have realistic and attainable goals. Show me how to balance my life for today while at the same time planning for tomorrow. Remind me to set my eyes on You so I can see where we're going together, with my future on the horizon.

....

....

....

....

....

Morning

DON'T TOUCH MY FEET

Jesus answered, "Unless I wash you, you have no part with me."
JOHN 13:8 NIV

Lord, I'm thinking about foot washing. The idea of having someone—especially You—wash *my* feet makes me squirm. That is appalling grace, like Your offering Yourself up on the cross for us, an act of love so unbelievable that I sometimes don't know what to do with it. How can I thank You adequately for that? I don't think I ever can. Please take away the embarrassment and pride that so often keep me from running to You for the cleansing I desperately need. Amen.

....

....

....

....

Evening

A HABIT OF SELFLESSNESS

Since Christ suffered while he was in his body, strengthen yourselves with the same way of thinking Christ had. The person who has suffered in the body is finished with sin.
1 PETER 4:1 NCV

Lord, I've been self-centered. There are times when I felt like the world revolved around me. Forgive me for such selfishness. I won't die if everything doesn't go my way. Help me not to react so emotionally when something doesn't turn out as I expected. Give me compassion for others and a sense of selflessness to serve them.

....

....

....

....

Morning

GROANING

*In the same way, the Spirit helps us in our weakness. We
do not know what we ought to pray for, but the Spirit
himself intercedes for us through wordless groans.*

ROMANS 8:26 NIV

Dear Lord, my heart and my mind feel empty right now. I don't know how
or what to pray. I feel like a great weight is sitting on my chest, and I'm
afraid the only thing that's going to come out is a horrible noise filled with
tears and tiredness. Thank You for knowing that I am weak and wordless.
Thank You for Your Spirit, my Comforter. Speak for me. Amen.

....

....

....

....

Evening

LOOKING FORWARD

*When the Spirit of truth comes, he will guide you into all
truth. He will not speak on his own but will tell you
what he has heard. He will tell you about the future.*

JOHN 16:13 NLT

Sometimes I look back at the things that didn't turn out quite right for me.
I know I shouldn't focus on wrongs done to me or opportunities missed.
You have set a great life before me, and I want to embrace it without the
shadow of the past. Help me see the future with joy and expectation. My
hope is in *You*!

....

....

....

....

Morning

HOW'S THE SERVICE?

*"For the LORD searches all hearts and understands all the intent
of the thoughts. If you seek Him, He will be found by you."*

1 CHRONICLES 28:9 NKJV

Dear Lord, I try to serve daily. I am asking You to show me my heart. Is my service pleasing to You? Am I serving under obligation, as one who is a slave to sin? Or am I serving with the voluntary spirit of my freedom in Christ? I long to serve without counting the cost. Please show me who and how to serve, then help me do it in Jesus' name. Amen.

....

....

....

....

Evening

SHARING MY BLESSINGS

*"Everyone shall give as he is able, in accordance to the
blessing of the LORD your God which He has given you."*

DEUTERONOMY 16:17 NASB

Lord, You have blessed me and the works of my hands. I am so grateful. As You bless me, I am able to bless others in whatever way I can. What a feeling, knowing I can help expand Your kingdom! Help me tithe my talents, money, and time, all to Your glory. For thine is the kingdom and the power, forever and ever.

....

....

....

....

....

Morning

THE GLORY OF HIS NAME

Give unto the LORD the glory due unto his name:
bring an offering, and come into his courts.

PSALM 96:8 KJV

Lord, fill me with the glory of Your name. May I see the splendor and light of Your character everywhere I turn. When I am burdened, show me evidence of Your love in my daily interactions with others and with Your creation. I want to always be ready with God-filled responses to people who ask about my hope.

....

....

....

....

Evening

THE LAW OF SOWING AND REAPING

"Bring to the storehouse a full tenth of what you earn so there will be food
in my house. Test me in this," says the LORD All-Powerful. "I will open
the windows of heaven for you and pour out all the blessings you need."

MALACHI 3:10 NCV

Lord, I give of myself to bless others because that is what You have called me to do. The more I step out in Your Word, the more I am blessed by Your presence and promises. I am focused on the spiritual, for that is what keeps me close to You, unshaken, undisturbed. Praise Your holy name!

....

....

....

....

....

Morning

CHOOSING LIFE

*"I call heaven and earth as witnesses today against you,
that I have set before you life and death, blessing and cursing;
therefore choose life, that both you and your descendants may live."*

DEUTERONOMY 30:19 NKJV

Lord, today I choose life—I choose to live in You. Instead of looking at all I don't have, I look at all that You have blessed me with. . . . Lord, the list is endless. Thank You so much for being my life, today and every day! I cling to You, each and every moment. Live through me!

....

....

....

....

....

Evening

GET OUT OF JAIL FREE

Whosoever shall call on the name of the LORD shall be delivered.

JOEL 2:32 KJV

Father, the world tells me there's no such thing as a free pass. I need to pay my dues, and then someday I may (if I'm lucky) reap the reward. And of course my actions have consequences—the world is quick to remind me of this as well. But, Father, when I am in trouble—when my soul is in captivity—remind me that all I have to do is call Your name. . .and You will set me free.

....

....

....

....

Morning

MAJESTY AND STRENGTH

And he shall stand and feed in the strength of the LORD,
in the majesty of the name of the LORD his God.

MICAH 5:4 KJV

Lord, the stress of life and the burdens of this world often leave me feeling weak and powerless. But Your name is majesty and strength. Your name is higher, more powerful, and far more excellent than anything this world has to offer me. All I need to do is tap into the power of Your name, and You promise to sustain me. I can do all things through You because You give me strength!

....

....

....

....

Evening

HEAVENLY BLESSINGS

All praise to God, the Father of our Lord Jesus Christ,
who has blessed us with every spiritual blessing in the
heavenly realms because we are united with Christ.

EPHESIANS 1:3 NLT

Because I am united with Your Son, who gave His life so that we could live, You have blessed me with every spiritual blessing. I am at peace. I am blessed. I am in the heavenly realms. Here, nothing can harm me, for He has blessed me beyond measure. Lord, my cup runneth over with love for You!

....

....

....

....

....

Morning
THE HOLLOW

Keep me as the apple of your eye; hide me in the shadow of your wings.
PSALM 17:8 NIV

Jesus, when I think about You making Your home in my heart, I imagine a little creature padding a tree hollow with leaves, turning in a tight, furry circle, and falling asleep. The tree is strong and stands unbowed through the winter storms. I am that creature, Lord. You are the tree. It is not so much that You live in *me*, but that I live in *You*. Thank You for letting me burrow into Your deep, safe, warm heart, Lord. Amen.

....

....

....

....

....

Evening
MY JOB

*Do not do wrong to repay a wrong, and do not insult to repay
an insult. But repay with a blessing, because you yourselves
were called to do this so that you might receive a blessing.*
1 PETER 3:9 NCV

My job—to bless others. What an awesome privilege to be an extension of Your arm! To do these things in secret, not wanting to be known, fills me with so much pleasure. There is nothing like it. Show me whose lives I can bless today, even in the simplest of things.

....

....

....

....

Morning
SINGING GOD'S NAME

I will praise the name of God with a song,
and will magnify him with thanksgiving.
PSALM 69:30 KJV

God, fill me with Your song today. Orchestrate within my heart a melody that is truly a joyful noise, one that will bring gladness to Your heart. Give me words of praise for You and words of encouragement for others. Fill my song with Your peace and Your beauty. Help me live out that song every moment, regardless of my circumstances. May I hallow Your name with singing.

....

....

....

....

....

Evening
JOY

Our mouths were filled with laughter, our tongues with songs of joy.
PSALM 126:2 NIV

Lord, thank You for the gift of laughter! Thank You for the joy You bring into my life through a child's smile, a luscious peach, a hot bath, and a good night's sleep. Help me remember that when I am "looking up" to You, Lord, I can have a more optimistic outlook and be a more positive person. Keep my eyes on You, not on myself or my circumstances, so I can live with a lighter, more joy-filled heart.

....

....

....

....

Morning

IN QUIETNESS

For thus saith the Lord GOD, the Holy One of Israel; In returning and rest shall ye be saved; in quietness and in confidence shall be your strength.

ISAIAH 30:15 KJV

Lord, sometimes it feels like I never sit down. There are always so many things to do. The noise and busyness of my life seem unending. I know You call me to come to You in quietness and rest. That quietness and rest in Your presence is the source of my strength. Thank You for longing to protect my heart in this crazy, merry-go-round world. Amen.

....

....

....

....

Evening

PRAISE YE THE LORD

May the peoples praise you, God; may all the peoples praise you. The land yields its harvest; God, our God, blesses us.

PSALM 67:5–6 NIV

Praise God from whom all blessings flow. You bless us beyond measure. You give us green meadows in which to lie down, calm waters to give us rest. There is no greater blessing than Your presence, than Your desire to hear my troubles. You are here to lift the burden from my shoulders and shower blessings upon me. I praise the name of Jesus.

....

....

....

....

....

Morning

A DAILY BENEDICTION

*"The LORD bless you, and keep you; the LORD cause
His face to shine on you, and be gracious to you;
the LORD lift up His face to you, and give you peace."*
NUMBERS 6:24–26 NASB

May You walk down the road with me today. Bless me and keep me from danger. May Your light keep me from the darkness surrounding me. Give me grace and peace and strength for the day. Give me someone to bless as You have blessed me. May You be there, waiting for me, at the end of the day.

....

....

....

....

Evening

A GOD OF JUSTICE

For I the LORD love judgment, I hate robbery.
ISAIAH 61:8 KJV

If I hallow Your name, God, then I need to remember just who You really are: a God of justice. Remind me that You have called me to show the same justice in everything I do. Thank You for being the perfect balance of justice and mercy, of fairness and love. Try as I might, I cannot strike that balance in my life without Your help. Teach me to love justice and strive for justice every day.

....

....

....

....

....

Morning

FACE TO GRACE

And He said to me, "My grace is sufficient for you, for My strength is made perfect in weakness." Therefore most gladly I will rather boast in my infirmities, that the power of Christ may rest upon me.

2 CORINTHIANS 12:9 NKJV

Father, my friend who loves You is dying. I praise You, Lord, because the power of Christ is so visibly resting on her right now. Only You can do this: give a dying woman a joy and strength that evangelizes *others*. She is giving You all the glory. And I am seeing Your wonders. Amen.

....

....

....

....

....

Evening

THE HEALING EDGE

People. . .begged him to let the sick just touch the edge of his cloak, and all who touched him were healed.

MATTHEW 14:35–36 NIV

Lord, when I connect with You, when my body is filled with Your power and love, nothing can harm me. I am healed from within. Fill me now with Your presence. Heal my body, soul, and spirit. I praise Your name, for You are the one who heals me, saves me, loves me! Thank You for giving me life!

....

....

....

....

....

Morning
CALLED BY HIS NAME

Thy words were found, and I did eat them; and thy word was unto me the joy and rejoicing of mine heart: for I am called by thy name, O LORD God of hosts.

JEREMIAH 15:16 KJV

God, not only have You adopted me as Your child, but You say I also have Your name as my own. You pursued me, You purchased me, You accepted me, You love me. Although I don't deserve the honor of being called Yours, I am so happy to accept the gift. Help me strive to be worthy of it.

....

....

....

....

....

Evening
OBEDIENCE AND BLESSINGS

Obey the LORD your God so that all these blessings will come and stay with you.

DEUTERONOMY 28:2 NCV

I hear Your voice, Lord, and I thank You for the blessings You have showered upon me. You love me so much that at times I cannot understand it. All that You have blessed me with goes beyond me, as I respond to Your voice, do Your will, and work to serve others. Speak to me, Lord. Tell me whom, what, and where You want me to bless. I am Your servant, Lord; speak to me.

....

....

....

....

....

Morning

STRENGTH IN JOY

*Nehemiah said, "Go and enjoy choice food and sweet drinks,
and send some to those who have nothing prepared. This day is holy
to our Lord. Do not grieve, for the joy of the LORD is your strength."*

NEHEMIAH 8:10 NIV

So often, Lord, I complain about how much work I have to do, how little
I am appreciated, how relentlessly hard life seems. But You tell me in this
verse to do these things: eat, drink, and share with others. Since Jesus came
to earth, every day is a celebration. Your festival-joy is the strength I need
to keep on. Amen.

....

....

....

....

Evening

PUTTING GOD FIRST

*No man can serve two masters: for either he will hate
the one, and love the other; or else he will hold to the one,
and despise the other. Ye cannot serve God and mammon.*

MATTHEW 6:24 KJV

Father, a glance at my bank statement causes me to shudder. Where does my
money go? Am I too concerned with what the world says I must possess to
be cool, to fit in, to appear successful? Your Word says that I cannot serve
both material wealth and You. I choose You, Lord. Be the master of my life
and of my checkbook. I need Your help with this. Amen.

....

....

....

....

Morning
SO BE IT

The effective, fervent prayer of a righteous man avails much.
JAMES 5:16 NKJV

Dearest Lord, I can't see the future. I know what I think would be best for me and the people around me, but I don't have Your eyes. So I pray, but I hold my prayers lightly. Are they Your will? Show me, Lord. When I pray *Amen*, I think what I really mean is *Your will be done*. I long to obey with knowledge, but for now I will simply obey. And wait on You. Amen.

....

....

....

....

....

Evening
STRENGTH IN WEAKNESS

Therefore I take pleasure in infirmities, in reproaches, in needs, in persecutions, in distresses, for Christ's sake. For when I am weak, then I am strong.
2 CORINTHIANS 12:10 NKJV

It's a paradox, but it is Your truth. When I am weak, I am strong because Your strength is made perfect in my weakness. Because You are in my life, I can rest in You. With Your loving arms around me, I am buoyed in spirit, soul, and body. When I am with You there is peace and comfort.

....

....

....

....

....

....

Morning

EATING GOD'S HOLINESS

That we might be partakers of his holiness.
HEBREWS 12:10 KJV

Father, I honor Your name by taking my fill each day of Your holiness. Make Your Spirit alive and active in my heart today. Remind me to always seek You through prayer, meditation on Your Word, and simply being still in Your presence. And when I get "too busy" to take the time to spend with You, please invite me back into Your presence. I can't handle life on my own. . . nor do I want to.

....

....

....

....

Evening

I WANT TO BE LIKE JESUS

And we know that in all things God works for the good of those who love him, who have been called according to his purpose. For those God foreknew he also predestined to be conformed to the image of his Son.
ROMANS 8:28–29 NIV

Lord, I know You will work everything out according to Your will. I feel privileged that You have chosen me to serve You. I want to be like You. Give me the strength of Christ, for His grace is sufficient for me. Thank You for hearing my prayer. O my soul, rejoice!

....

....

....

....

....

Morning
IN A DRY TIME

On the last and greatest day of the festival, Jesus stood and said in a loud voice, "Let anyone who is thirsty come to me and drink. Whoever believes in me, as Scripture has said, rivers of living water will flow from within them."
JOHN 7:37–38 NIV

Dear Father, I want to pray, but the words will not come. You tell me in Your Word that if I come to You, streams of living water will flow from within me. Thank You for that promise. I am assured that this dry time will not last if I come to You for refreshing. I am waiting on You.

....

....

....

....

Evening
TO YIELD TO GOD'S STANDARDS

I urge you, as foreigners and exiles, to abstain from sinful desires, which wage war against your soul.
1 PETER 2:11 NIV

Lord, You know me better than I know myself. You know the things that challenge me deep within my soul. You know what I need. I surrender what I want for what You know I need. You have the highest standards, and I want to meet them. I give myself to Your will and hope with great expectation to live my life according to the standards You have set in place.

....

....

....

....

....

Morning
LIGHT

God is light, and in him is no darkness at all.
1 JOHN 1:5 KJV

Father God, Your name is light. You have no darkness in Your character. Your brilliance is dazzling—brighter than the brightest star and more beautiful than the most awe-inspiring celestial display. You are a hope-filled promise of never-ending illumination. Please shine on me—and shine *through* me so that others may see the darkness of this world flee before Your light.

....

....

....

....

....

Evening
DISSUADED FROM YOUR GOAL

They were just trying to intimidate us, imagining that they could discourage us and stop the work. So I continued the work with even greater determination.
NEHEMIAH 6:9 NLT

Lord, people are trying to intimidate me, telling me there is no way I can meet the challenge You have set before me. But I have faith in You. I know I can do whatever You call me to do. Help me avoid letting others dissuade me from my goal. Give me the faith that David sought from You, the kind that does not waver but goes boldly forward.

....

....

....

....

....

Morning
THE ROCK

The LORD is my rock, and my fortress, and my deliverer;
my God, my strength, in whom I will trust; my buckler,
and the horn of my salvation, and my high tower.
PSALM 18:2 KJV

So many names You have, Lord: Rock, Fortress, Deliverer, Buckler, Horn of
Salvation, High Tower. All of them tell me that I can trust You absolutely.
All of them tell me You are in control, that You will shield me from danger,
that I shouldn't be afraid, that I am safe in Your mighty hand. You will
never let me down.

....

....

....

....

Evening
FEARLESSNESS

Though an army may encamp against me, my heart shall not fear.
PSALM 27:3 NKJV

I remember the story of David, how he faced opposition under the watchful
eye of his enemies. But he was not afraid. Oh, that I would have such faith.
Sometimes I get so scared that my heart begins beating a mile a minute.
Those are the times when I have taken my eyes off You. Keep my focus on
Your Word. Plant this verse in my heart so that when dread comes upon
me, I can say these words and kiss fear goodbye.

....

....

....

....

....

Morning
DINNER AT JESUS' HOUSE

"Behold, I stand at the door and knock; if anyone hears My voice and opens the door, I will come in to him and will dine with him, and he with Me."

REVELATION 3:20 NASB

Father, Your Word says that Jesus didn't have a home of His own. His home was wherever on the road He happened to be when night fell. Today it hit me that my home is Jesus' home too. I ask Your blessing, Lord, as I seek to understand what that kind of house is like. I ask for Your grace and power to be real in our lives, *here*. Amen.

....

....

....

....

Evening
SUPPORT OF FELLOW BELIEVERS

When [Paul] would not be dissuaded, we gave up and said, "The Lord's will be done."

ACTS 21:14 NIV

Sometimes people think believers like me are crazy. We're not. We just know that when You call us to do something, we are to go forward with no fear. We are bold in You, Lord! Fellow believers encourage us, knowing that if it is Your will, then all will be well. What would I do without that support? Thank You for planting my feet in a nice broad place, surrounded by fellow believers who love and pray for me.

....

....

....

....

....

Morning
GUARANTEED BLESSING

"The LORD will guarantee a blessing on everything you do."
DEUTERONOMY 28:8 NLT

Your Word says that You actually *guarantee* a blessing on everything I do! That's a promise I can count on. It gives me confidence that You will be with me in all that I do, blessing me at each and every turn. What an awesome promise! I arise today, assured of Your assistance, guidance, and approval of every good thing. No words can express how You make me feel. I am humbled in Your presence and renewed in Your light. I praise You, Lord!

....

....

....

....

Evening
TRUTH

Lead me in thy truth, and teach me: for thou art the
God of my salvation; on thee do I wait all the day.
PSALM 25:5 KJV

Your Son said He was the Way, the Truth, and the Life. Father, may I always walk in Your truth, the truth of Jesus. Teach me patience as I wait for You to move, to act in my life, as I wait for Your return. Waiting is not an easy thing to do, God. Please give me the strength to trust in the hope of my salvation in You. Your truth means everything to me.

....

....

....

....

....

Morning
OUT OF SIGHT

*And when he was demanded of the Pharisees, when the
kingdom of God should come, he answered them and said,
The kingdom of God cometh not with observation.*

LUKE 17:20 KJV

Father, I can't always see the reality of Your kingdom in the world around me. Give me eyes of faith. Show me the people who are working for Your goals, and give me the opportunity to serve alongside them. Allow me to bring Your kingdom to the people and places around me that need You most.

....

....

....

....

....

Evening
OUR HELP

Our help is in the name of the LORD, who made heaven and earth.

PSALM 124:8 NKJV

I need look no further than You, Lord, to help me. It is Your name that I trust. Your power will help me meet this challenge. You know the plan for my life. You have equipped me to do what You have called me to do. Help me rely on You and Your power. That is what will give me victory in this life. Thank You for hearing and answering my prayer.

....

....

....

....

....

Morning

LIVING SACRIFICES

Therefore, I urge you, brothers and sisters, in view of God's mercy, to offer your bodies as a living sacrifice, holy and pleasing to God—this is your true and proper worship.

Romans 12:1 NIV

Lord, I lift myself up to You this morning. I live to please You, for I love You with all my strength, soul, mind, heart, and body. I dedicate my time and service to You. Show me the path You want me to take so that at the end of my days, when I see Your smiling face, You will say, *"She did what she could."*

....

....

....

....

Evening

DETOURS ON THE WAY TO AMEN

Strengthened with all might, according to his glorious power, unto all patience and longsuffering with joyfulness.

Colossians 1:11 KJV

Father, quiet times are more like dull-roar times in my busy home. But when I study Your Word, Lord, I am often so surprised: Jesus going off alone into the wilderness to pray, then being followed by the disciples who couldn't seem to get enough of Him. They interrupted His prayers, and He never once sent them away. So thank You for the interruptions, Lord; I'm welcoming them as a chance to be like Jesus. Conform my character. Amen.

....

....

....

....

Morning

GOOD NEWS

*He went throughout every city and village, preaching
and shewing the glad tidings of the kingdom of God.*

LUKE 8:1 KJV

Make me Your ambassador, Lord, carrying the good news of Your kingdom
to everyone I meet today. Give me new opportunities and new relationships
that I might not normally notice, so I can reach more hearts for You. Help
me see these individuals through Your eyes, as loved children of God, created
in Your image. Give me the right words to say, and open their ears so they
can truly understand the glad tidings of Your kingdom.

....

....

....

....

Evening

MY ARMOR

*I will not trust in my bow, nor shall my sword save me. But You have
saved us from our enemies, and have put to shame those who hated
us. In God we boast all day long, and praise Your name forever.*

PSALM 44:6–8 NKJV

My power is in the faith-based boldness that only comes from knowing
You intimately. With that weapon in my arsenal, there is only victory ahead.
I want to bring glory to you. It is in You that I boast all day long. I praise
Your name, my Strength and my Deliverer.

....

....

....

....

....

Morning
STANDING WITH GOD

Everyone deserted me. May it not be held against them. But the Lord
stood at my side and gave me strength. . . . And I was delivered.
2 TIMOTHY 4:16–17 NIV

Lord, I am not going to be mad at others for deserting me. I don't need them. All I need is You. You are my Lord, my Savior, my Deliverer, my Rock, my Refuge. You are by my side. I can feel Your presence. Oh, how wonderful You are! Thank You for giving me the power I need. Thank You for never leaving me.

....

....

....

....

Evening
TRAIL SIGNS

Your ears shall hear a word behind you, saying, "This is the way, walk in
it," whenever you turn to the right hand or whenever you turn to the left.
ISAIAH 30:21 NKJV

Dear God, I just want to thank You for speaking to me through another believer and keeping me from sin. Lord, You know how I longed to send that email and share something I shouldn't have. I was about to gossip, and I'm sorry. I'm so glad You sent someone to stand behind me and read over my shoulder and gently tell me not to hit SEND. Amen.

....

....

....

....

....

Morning

RIGHTEOUSNESS, PEACE, AND JOY

For the kingdom of God is not meat and drink; but
righteousness, and peace, and joy in the Holy Ghost.
ROMANS 14:17 KJV

Remind me, Father, that Your kingdom is not built on the things of this world. The truth is that Your kingdom flies in the face of the things of the world. Righteousness, peace, and joy are heavenly attributes that we humans have a difficult time living out without Your Spirit to change our hearts. May I not depend on external reality for my satisfaction, instead dwelling always in Your realm of peace and joy.

....

....

....

....

....

Evening

HOPE

"And now, Lord, what do I wait for? My hope is in You."
PSALM 39:7 NKJV

I hope in You and what You want to do through me while I'm here on earth. Don't let me drag my feet in fear, but let me boldly run forward as David did when he faced Goliath. David knew You, and he knew that You would always be with him, no matter what. That's a fabulous faith. That's faith-based boldness! Empower me with that today so that I, like David, can go out with You and take on giants.

....

....

....

....

Morning
THE SOWER

And he said, So is the kingdom of God, as if
a man should cast seed into the ground.

MARK 4:26 KJV

God, what does this mean: Your kingdom is like a man casting seed on the ground? Does this mean I can find Your kingdom everywhere, scattered throughout our world by Your generous hand? Give me new eyes to see Your kingdom all around me, especially in places I wouldn't expect to see You. Father, thank You for Your generosity. Thank You that You do not ever withhold Yourself but are always giving.

....

....

....

....

Evening
MAKE ME BOLD

On the day I called, You answered me; You
made me bold with strength in my soul.

PSALM 138:3 NASB

Sometimes I feel like a weakling when it comes to my faith. I let my doubts and fears overtake me and then find myself shrinking from the challenges You put before me. Lord, I ask You to make me bold. Give me the strength to do what You want me to do. Dispel the darkness that surrounds me. Warm me with Your light. Bring me where You want me to be. Give me strength in my soul!

....

....

....

....

Morning

FASTER, DONKEY?

"Be still, and know that I am God."
PSALM 46:10 NIV

Jesus, did You ever hurry? Did You ever kick Your heels into the donkey's side so it would trot just a bit faster? I don't think so. Your Word shows You differently: wherever You were was exactly where You wanted to be at that moment. I long to be like that. Help me slow down and savor my life: the small moments of glory, quiet words with a friend, even the daily struggles that are conforming me to Your image. I am *here*, and so are You. Amen.

....

....

....

....

Evening

BY FAITH, I GO

*By faith Abraham, when he was called, obeyed by going
out to a place which he was to receive for an inheritance;
and he left, not knowing where he was going.*
HEBREWS 11:8 NASB

What Abraham might have given for a map! But that's what faith is all about. It's the substance of things hoped for, the evidence of things unseen (see Hebrews 11:1). So give me that faith, Lord. By faith I will obey this call You have put upon my life. I will go out, not knowing, because I trust in You!

....

....

....

....

....

Morning
A MUSTARD SEED

*The kingdom of God. . . .is like a grain of mustard seed, which, when
it is sown in the earth, is less than all the seeds that be in the earth.*
MARK 4:30–31 KJV

Lord, in order for Your kingdom to grow and expand, please plant a seed
of faith in my heart. Make my heart a fertile place for that faith to grow
so that my work in Your kingdom will be fruitful. Embolden Your Spirit
in me so that I might contribute greatly to Your plans—not for my glory
but for Yours alone, Father.

Evening
GOD LOOKS AT THE HEART

*But the LORD said to Samuel, "Do not consider his appearance or his height,
for I have rejected him. The LORD does not look at the things people look at.
People look at the outward appearance, but the LORD looks at the heart."*
1 SAMUEL 16:7 NIV

With You I can do anything, Lord. I know that You have made me to use
my talents to accomplish specific tasks here on earth. You know my purpose,
my path. Help me use all my resources to meet this challenge before me.
All to Your glory!

Morning
BEFORE THE DOORBELL RINGS

*All the days of the afflicted are evil, but he
who is of a merry heart has a continual feast.*
PROVERBS 15:15 NKJV

Dear Lord, I so wanted to have some quiet moments with You this morning, but the day is rushing at me quickly. I am still going to choose joy today, Lord. I am going to choose to take what You give with open arms. I can pray where I stand, as I walk and talk; I can meditate on Your Word in any and every situation. And maybe I can get up earlier tomorrow! Amen.

....

....

....

....

....

Evening
DARING TO DREAM

Take delight in the LORD, and he will give you the desires of your heart.
PSALM 37:4 NIV

God, I believe you've placed dreams within me that are yet to be realized. Teach me to delight myself in You as I pursue the desires of my heart. Show me Your perfect will—may I move as far and as fast as you wish, never less or more. Grant me the wisdom I need to accomplish Your plans for my life and the humility to give You the glory in them.

....

....

....

....

....

Morning
AT THE THRONE

So let us come boldly to the throne of our gracious God. There we will receive his mercy, and we will find grace to help us when we need it most.
HEBREWS 4:16 NLT

Lord, I need Your mercy this morning. Help me resist running from this challenge. Give me the grace, strength, energy, talent, and intelligence that I need to make this come out right. I come to You, bowing down, asking for Your love and power to fill me and give me the strength I need to accomplish the challenges before me today.

....

....

....

....

Evening
LIKE A CHILD

Verily I say unto you, Whosoever shall not receive the kingdom of God as a little child, he shall not enter therein.
MARK 10:15 KJV

Give me a child's heart, Lord. Create in me the simple and heartfelt belief that You celebrate and cherish in Your children. Let me experience the wonder of Your love and gift of grace. Help me share with others, with childlike exuberance, the hope I have in You. Let me set aside grown-up worries and live a joyful life so that I can enter Your kingdom.

....

....

....

....

....

Morning

THE GOOD WORDS

Then our mouth was filled with laughter, and our tongue with singing.
Then they said among the nations, "The LORD has done great things for them."
PSALM 126:2 NKJV

You have filled my mouth with laughter! My tongue is singing Your praises!
I am so alive in You this morning. And it is because I am allowing You to
live in me and am putting Your Word into action. It can't get any better
than this, and it's all because of Your sacrifice. Thank You, Jesus, for making
me whole and happy in You!

....

....

....

....

....

Evening

MORE THAN JUST TALK

For the kingdom of God is not in word, but in power.
1 CORINTHIANS 4:20 KJV

God, I talk a good game, but sometimes my heart and actions don't carry
it through. Remind me that Your kingdom is active and powerful. It's not
just a bunch of talk. It's real, and it's here on earth now. You ask me to help
build Your kingdom; show me new ways to serve. Give me a passion for
Your kingdom on earth—and for Your heavenly kingdom as well.

....

....

....

....

....

Morning

KNOWING GOD'S WILL

Do not conform to the pattern of this world, but be transformed by the renewing of your mind. Then you will be able to test and approve what God's will is—his good, pleasing and perfect will.

Romans 12:2 NIV

Lord, I commit my aspirations to You. Give me courage to work toward my goals. Renew my mind and spirit so I can know Your will. I know You bring people and circumstances into my life for a reason. Thank You for the assurance that You will direct me into Your good purposes.

....

....

....

....

....

Evening

AFTER THE AMEN

"Who among all these does not know that the hand of the LORD has done this, in whose hand is the life of every living thing, and the breath of all mankind?"

Job 12:9–10 NASB

Father, how do I live once I get up off my knees? I like quick fixes that promise to solve problems in three easy steps. But I know You are not like that. What You've shown me most clearly, Lord, is to not wait for everything to be "perfect" before I follow You more faithfully. Help me to *live* as though I'm on my knees. Amen.

....

....

....

....

Morning
WHO HOLDS THE REINS?

All the ways of a man are pure in his own eyes, but the
LORD weighs the spirits. Commit your works to the
LORD, and your thoughts will be established.
PROVERBS 16:2–3 NKJV

Dear Father, I spend so much time trying to control others. I know that is not what You want. I can only control my own heart, Lord. I can't be the "holy spirit" of anyone else's heart. Please help me let go of my agenda and instead lift others up to You. Work on and through *me*, Lord, so they would be drawn closer to You. Amen.

....

....

....

....

Evening
THE GOD WHO CARES

You discern my going out and my lying down;
you are familiar with all my ways.
PSALM 139:3 NIV

Lord, I thank You that You are the God who cares! You want the best for me, and You are constantly designing the next steps of this journey of my life. Powerful, yet gentle and kind, You delight in giving us dreams—and the resources to achieve our goals. I pray for dreams that are worthy and wonderful. Empower me, gracious God, to be a woman of action who trusts You.

....

....

....

....

....

Morning
BLESSED POVERTY

Blessed be ye poor: for yours is the kingdom of God.
LUKE 6:20 KJV

Lord, make me willing to be poor in this world so that I can be rich in Your kingdom. Give me a spirit of generosity, even to the point where I give beyond my comfort level so that I must sacrifice my feelings of security. The things of earth are not the important things, God. I know You will take care of me, and You promise me an even greater reward in heaven.

....

....

....

....

....

Evening
THE GIVER OF GUIDANCE

*I will instruct you and teach you in the way you should
go; I will counsel you with my loving eye on you.*
PSALM 32:8 NIV

Lord, I appreciate Your wise hand of guidance. You teach me in the way I should go; You counsel me and watch over me. No one knows my inner heart and life dreams like You, Lord. Still me. Help me listen so I can hear Your direction. When I hear, give me the courage to walk forward knowing You are always near. You are with me every step of the way.

....

....

....

....

....

Morning

FALLING INTO LIGHT

Therefore He says: "Awake, you who sleep, arise
from the dead, and Christ will give you light."

EPHESIANS 5:14 NKJV

Dear Lord, again I thank You for Your precious Word. When I fall to my knees, You will strengthen me. I fall, Lord, because I am weak and You are great, and then in falling, miraculously, Your strength becomes mine. You dwell in me. Your boundless love bears fruit in me: enough both to keep and to give away. I—weak, broken, sin scarred, blind—am strong, whole, pure, clear eyed, and filled with the fullness of God. Praise God!

Evening

TRUSTING GOD'S WISDOM

For the LORD gives wisdom; from his mouth
come knowledge and understanding.

PROVERBS 2:6 NIV

Lord, what a blessing it is to be able to come before You—the wisest, most intelligent Being in the universe. I have direct access, straight to the top. Thank You for giving me wisdom and direction, even when I can't see the way. Knowledge and understanding come directly from Your mouth, Lord, and You delight to enlighten us. I praise You and ask for continued insight as my dreams become achievable goals.

Morning

DEAD AND GONE

Jesus said unto him, Let the dead bury their dead:
but go thou and preach the kingdom of God.

LUKE 9:60 KJV

God, help me to let go of the past and look instead to Your future. I ask You to be my Savior that covers my past sin, to lead me in Your will in my present circumstance, and to be with me as I move into Your future. May I not be preoccupied with that which is dead and gone; fill my thoughts and conversation with the reality of Your kingdom in the here and now.

....

....

....

....

....

Evening

NOTHING IS TOO HARD FOR GOD

"I am the LORD, the God of all mankind. Is anything too hard for me?"

JEREMIAH 32:27 NIV

Lord, there are so many obstacles. I need energy and motivation. More than anything, I need to trust You more. Nothing is too difficult for You, Father. You can do anything! Despite all my needs and distractions, please bring into my life favor and openings—please make a way. I ask that You would help me achieve the goals in my life that are best suited for Your good purposes.

....

....

....

....

Morning

CLEAN HOUSE

*So that He might sanctify the church, having cleansed
her by the washing of water with the word [of God].*
EPHESIANS 5:26 AMP

Dear God, my house is so messy. I just don't seem to have time to clean everything. Please help me be content with imperfection, because sometimes it seems like I can either clean or read Your Word, but not both. And I know it is far more important to wash the house of my soul with Your living water. Amen.

....

....

....

....

Evening

TRUSTING GOD'S PLANS FOR MY LIFE

*"For I know the plans I have for you," declares the LORD, "plans to
prosper you and not to harm you, plans to give you hope and a future."*
JEREMIAH 29:11 NIV

Lord, You are faithful. I have hope for my future because of Your promises. Reveal Your good plans for my life. As I share my dreams and visions with You, please mold them into reality—or mash them like clay on a potter's wheel into something more than I could ever have imagined. I put my trust in You, Lord.

....

....

....

....

....

Morning
HEALING

And heal the sick that are therein, and say unto them,
The kingdom of God is come nigh unto you.
LUKE 10:9 KJV

Your kingdom, Lord, brings healing to those who are sick in spirit, mind, or body. Help me carry Your healing to those around me. Remind me to not just *say* that I will pray for others who are sick but to earnestly and intentionally come to You on their behalf. Help me see the healing miracles You supply every moment of every day. Remind me to point others to Your goodness in those situations.

....

....

....

....

Evening
GOD IS FAITHFUL

The one who calls you is faithful, and he will do it.
1 THESSALONIANS 5:24 NIV

Lord, I thank You that You are faithful. No one else is like You. People move away, jobs change, and much of life is uncertain. But You are always here, my stable, loving, and present Lord. Help me hold unswervingly to the hope I profess, for You alone are faithful. You keep all Your promises—every one of them, all the time—and I thank You for that, Lord.

....

....

....

....

....

Morning
SANCTIFICATION

For this is the will of God, even your sanctification.

1 THESSALONIANS 4:3 KJV

God, Ruler of my life, You want me to be sanctified—wholly, utterly given to You. I surrender myself to Your will. I give You my heart, my family relationships, my friend relationships, my career, my ministry, my hobbies, my health. Gently prod me along to continue to surrender every area of my life to You—especially the ones that I try so desperately to take back and control on my own. Amen.

....

....

....

....

Evening
SURRENDERING MY DREAMS

*Going a little farther, he fell with his face to the ground
and prayed, "My Father, if it is possible, may this cup
be taken from me. Yet not as I will, but as you will."*

MATTHEW 26:39 NIV

Lord, I bow before You and give You my dreams. I surrender my will for Yours. When I am tempted to do things my way, may I seek Your guidance instead. Give me mercy to see that Your grace has everything covered. I don't have to be afraid, Lord. I will trust You to meet my every need.

....

....

....

....

....

Morning
THANKS

In every thing give thanks: for this is the will of God.
1 Thessalonians 5:18 kjv

King of the universe, I give You thanks for all You have given me. Thanks for the health You've granted that allows me to wake up feeling alert and refreshed. Thank You for the food that nourishes my body to do Your work. Thank You for the clothes You have provided to keep me warm. Thank You for work to do so I may glorify You. Continue to fill my heart with gratitude so that I may do Your will in the world.

....

....

....

....

Evening
TO KNOW YOU, LORD

I want you to show love, not offer sacrifices. I want you to know me more than I want burnt offerings.
Hosea 6:6 nlt

Heavenly Father, I am Your child. I want to know You more. Give me understanding of who You are and what You are like. Teach me the things that are important to You so they can become important to me. Help me put You first in my life. Give me wisdom to choose time with You and to eliminate distractions that keep me too busy for You.

....

....

....

....

....

Morning

WORDS, WORDS, WORDS

As newborn babes, desire the pure milk of the word, that you may grow thereby, if indeed you have tasted that the LORD is gracious.

1 PETER 2:2–3 NKJV

Father, my life is so full of words. I am bombarded by them (and bombard others with mine) all day long. How many of them really glorify You? That *is* my desire, Lord: to glorify You. Help me filter from the filth and froth what is pure and gracious. Help me desire truly to drink only Your pure milk so that it would flow out through me. Amen.

....

....

....

....

....

Evening

KNOWING THE TRUTH

We know also that the Son of God has come and has given us understanding, so that we may know him who is true. And we are in him who is true by being in his Son Jesus Christ. He is the true God and eternal life.

1 JOHN 5:20 NIV

Lord, thank You for making absolute truth available. You came into the world to testify for truth. It is not relative to what I think or feel. Truth is objective and based on Your Word. Help me know the truth and see it clearly in my life.

....

....

....

....

Morning
DELIGHT

I delight to do thy will, O my God.
PSALM 40:8 KJV

Thank You, God, that Your will is not one of sadness and gloom. I am grateful that You are not a God that relishes seeing Your children suffer. In fact, You take great pleasure in giving good gifts to me! What a joy to know that You think of me in that way! As I learn to live always within Your kingdom, I am delighted to be able to give back in some small way as I serve You and others.

....

....

....

....

....

Evening
GOD AND EMOTIONS

"The LORD is slow to anger, abounding in love and forgiving sin and rebellion."
NUMBERS 14:18 NIV

Lord, what a blessing that You have given us such an array of emotions with which to express ourselves. Help me be more like You—slow to anger and abounding in love. Help me be a woman who is forgiving. I pray for more discernment so that in whatever comes my way I will have the grace to think, speak, and act with a good and godly attitude.

....

....

....

....

Morning

TIME FOR HEALING

He heals the brokenhearted and binds up their wounds.

PSALM 147:3 NASB

Dear Lord, I find myself obsessing over certain people who upset me. I think about how they have wounded me, and those wounds become deeper and sadder. Lord, when I do this, I am not letting Jesus come into these situations and offer His gifts of forgiveness and healing. Please forgive me for relishing my wounds more than Your healing. Help me pray *for* people instead of muttering against them. I want to know You, Lord, and the power of Your resurrection, even in my small hurts. Amen.

....

....

....

....

Evening

LOVE FOR OTHERS

Dear friends, let us love one another, for love comes from God.
Everyone who loves has been born of God and knows God.

1 JOHN 4:7 NIV

Lord, You are the author of love. As I read Your Word and discover what love really is, help me express that love for others. You are so good at loving people—You are kind, compassionate, interested, accepting, and nonjudgmental. You seek the best for others. You empathize with their joy and sadness. You make them feel special. Lord, let me be a person who loves like that.

....

....

....

....

Morning
FOREVER

And the world passeth away, and the lust thereof:
but he that doeth the will of God abideth for ever.
1 JOHN 2:17 KJV

The things of this world never last. I don't know why I get excited about acquiring material things. The anticipation is better than the real thing, which always ends in disappointment. Even my cravings for this world's things come and go. Thank You, Lord God, that Your kingdom is permanent, and I will dwell there forever. Give me a passion for eternity with You—payoff that absolutely will not disappoint!

....

....

....

....

Evening
PATIENCE FOR IN "THE MEANTIME"

Be patient, then, brothers and sisters, until the Lord's coming.
See how the farmer waits for the land to yield its valuable
crop, patiently waiting for the autumn and spring rains.
JAMES 5:7 NIV

Lord, it's hard to wait. There are so many things I want. But You give us the "meantime" season for a reason. I ask for the patience and courage to wait well. Help me be a woman of wisdom. You are not just killing time, Lord—You are ordering events and shaping my character. I yield to Your timing, Father.

....

....

....

....

Morning

FIRST THINGS FIRST

But seek ye first the kingdom of God, and his righteousness;
and all these things shall be added unto you.

MATTHEW 6:33 KJV

You understand, Lord, that I have bills to pay, deadlines to meet, a house to clean, a family to care for. These things are important, but they don't have ultimate importance. Remind me always to seek Your kingdom ahead of all these things. Give me a life of balance that is faithfully committed to Your call. Help me trust that You will take care of (and bless) the details of my life.

....

....

....

....

....

Evening

CONFIDENCE

Have no fear of sudden disaster or of the ruin that overtakes the wicked, for
the LORD will be at your side and will keep your foot from being snared.

PROVERBS 3:25–26 NIV

Lord, I want to be more confident. Give me the courage to know that You, Lord, will be my confidence. Even when I say the wrong thing, You have the power to make things right again. Thank You for the confidence You give me. Let me walk with my head high because I know who I am in Christ: I am Yours!

....

....

....

....

Morning
JOY SCHOOL

"Come to Me, all who are weary and burdened, and I will give you rest. Take My yoke upon you and learn from Me, for I am gentle and humble in heart, and YOU WILL FIND REST FOR YOUR SOULS."
MATTHEW 11:28–29 NASB

Joy is not my native language, Lord. I am more fluent in complaint and bitterness. I long to speak like the angels at the dawn of creation when they all shouted for joy! This is what I would say: "You are good! You are holy! You are God!" Thank You for making me in Your image, so I can grow and change. Amen.

....

....

....

....

Evening
STRESS

Cast your cares on the LORD and he will sustain you; he will never let the righteous be shaken.
PSALM 55:22 NIV

Lord, I can't take one more day of this hectic whirl of life. Sometimes it just feels like too much! Help me breathe out my cares, casting them away like line from a fishing rod. Don't let me reel them back in! Here is my burned-out, anxious heart. May Your oceans of love and power replenish me, providing the energy I need to do what You want me to do each day.

....

....

....

....

....

Morning

AMAZING FORGIVENESS

In Him we have redemption through His blood, the
forgiveness of sins, according to the riches of His grace.

EPHESIANS 1:7 NKJV

Lord, I come into Your presence, thanking You for forgiveness. In a culture where many experience clinical depression because of guilt, I can know my past is redeemed because of Christ's sacrifice for me. Your forgiveness is so amazing. Although I don't deserve it, You pour it out freely and lovingly. Because You have seen fit to pardon me, I bless Your name today.

....

....

....

....

Evening

MY COMPANION

"Surely I am with you always, to the very end of the age."

MATTHEW 28:20 NIV

Lord, I thank You that You are my true companion—that I am never alone. You have assigned angels to watch over and protect me. You have given me your Holy Spirit and promised that You are with me always, even to the very end of the age. What a privilege that You call me Your friend. As we travel this road of life together, on city sidewalks, suburban roads, or country paths, I enjoy your presence, Lord. Help me never forget Your presence.

....

....

....

....

Morning
PATIENCE

*For ye have need of patience, that, after ye have
done the will of God, ye might receive the promise.*
HEBREWS 10:36 KJV

King of my heart, I want to do Your will. You know that sometimes, though, I grow impatient and filled with doubt. I am distracted by the temptations of the world—money, relationships, power, prestige—that look like answers to my problems. In my heart of hearts, I know they will only lead to ruin. Help me keep going, relying on You. I know You always keep Your promises.

....

....

....

....

Evening
HEALING GUILT AND SHAME

*I said, "I will confess my transgressions to the
LORD." And you forgave the guilt of my sin.*
PSALM 32:5 NIV

Lord, I can no longer hide in the darkness of my sin. You know everything I've done wrong, yet you bring me into the light—not to condemn me but to heal me. I acknowledge my wrongs and confess them all to You. I stand in Your forgiveness as the cleansing water of Your gentle love flows over me, washing away my guilt and shame.

....

....

....

....

....

Morning
HEART TRANSPLANT

*Therefore, if anyone is in Christ, the new creation
has come: The old has gone, the new is here!*
2 CORINTHIANS 5:17 NIV

Dear Father, You have blessed me with a healthy body, and I praise You for it. Many are not so blessed. But we all have hidden wounds, Father, wounds that bleed out onto other people. You know what mine are, even better than I do. You are the great Healer, Lord. You heal with a touch, with a word. You heal simply with Your presence. Show me my hurts, Lord, and heal them. Amen.

....

....

....

....

....

Evening
A NEW SONG

He put a new song in my mouth, a hymn of praise to our God.
PSALM 40:3 NIV

Lord, give me a new song to sing, a happier tune! I know there is no mess too big for You to fix, no broken life too shattered for You to restore, and no loss too great for You to redeem. As You raise me out of the darkness of my depression, lifting me to solid emotional ground, I will praise You.

....

....

....

....

....

Morning
ENOUGH

*God is able to make all grace abound toward you; that ye, always
having all sufficiency in all things, may abound to every good work.*

2 CORINTHIANS 9:8 KJV

You make me sufficient, Lord—You give me enough of everything I need—
to carry out Your will. Truth be told, You often supply *much more* than I
need. These blessings are wonderful surprises that I don't want to take for
granted. Show me ways that I can share Your blessings with others. You
are a good giver, Lord. Thank You.

....

....

....

....

....

Evening
PRAISE FOR GOD'S INDESCRIBABLE GIFT

*For God so loved the world that he gave his one and only Son,
that whoever believes in him shall not perish but have eternal life.*

JOHN 3:16 NIV

Thank You for giving the most precious gift, Your very own Son, so I could
live each day with You. There are no words to describe the depths of Your
sacrifice, but I know You did it for me. You gave Your only Son so You
could share life with many sons and daughters. I am so thankful Jesus was
willing to give His life for mine.

....

....

....

....

Morning
PROVISIONS FROM GOD

You open Your hand and satisfy the desire of every living thing.
PSALM 145:16 NKJV

God, there is no creature on earth You do not see or provide for. I'm bringing praise to You right now for the daily things You supply for me. It is through Your goodness that I have food, clothes, and water. Help me to always be thankful for what I have and to not emulate the wandering Israelites who, focusing on lack, preferred to complain. Your power is awesome; thank You for generously supplying my needs and wants each and every day.

....

....

....

....

....

Evening
TAKE UP YOUR CROSS

Then he said to the crowd, "If any of you wants to be my follower, you must give up your own way, take up your cross daily, and follow me."
LUKE 9:23 NLT

Jesus, it takes sacrifice to follow You. I have so many dreams for my life, but they are nothing unless they include You. Help me let go of the things I selfishly desire that aren't meant to be a part of my life. Your purposes for my life mean success. I give You my life—I completely surrender.

....

....

....

....

....

REST

For in six days the LORD made the heavens and the earth,
the sea, and all that is in them, and rested the seventh day.
Therefore the LORD blessed the Sabbath day and hallowed it.

EXODUS 20:11 NKJV

Dear Lord, rest does not come easily to me. I plan and work and *do*. Resting seems somehow self-indulgent and lazy. But Your thoughts toward me are numerous and higher than mine. You know what I need. Help me make my home and heart places of rest and worship. Show me what that means to You. Amen.

....

....

....

....

ASKING FOR GOD'S HELP

God is my helper; the Lord is with those who uphold my life.

PSALM 54:4 NKJV

Sometimes I think I should work things out on my own. I know I shouldn't feel like I'm bothering You, but my problems seem small compared to what others deal with. Still, I know You want to help me. You are just waiting for me to ask, so I'm asking—please help. You know what I'm dealing with. Forgive me for not coming to You sooner. I accept Your help today.

....

....

....

....

....

Morning

GOD'S RICHES

*My God shall supply all your need according
to his riches in glory by Christ Jesus.*

PHILIPPIANS 4:19 KJV

Why should I ever doubt Your ability to give me what I need, heavenly Father, when You have such riches? Your bounty is unfathomable, and You want to share it with me! How humbling! Help me remember that everything I call "mine" is actually Yours. Forgive me when my heart is hard and unwilling to accept Your riches in glory. Help me be open to Your Spirit as He moves in my heart.

....

....

....

....

Evening

STRENGTHENED IN THE FAITH

*Just as you received Christ Jesus as Lord, continue to live your
lives in him, rooted and built up in him, strengthened in the
faith as you were taught, and overflowing with thankfulness.*

COLOSSIANS 2:6–7 NIV

Jesus, thank You for always being with me, holding me up above the waters of this life, especially when the current is more than I can bear. As You uphold me, my faith grows. There is no one like You, Jesus. I am strengthened during this time with You. I overflow with thankfulness and praise. What would I ever do without You?

....

....

....

....

Morning
PRAY FOR ME

The LORD thunders at the head of his army; his forces are beyond number, and mighty is the army that obeys his command.
JOEL 2:11 NIV

Dear Lord, how many times have I told someone I would pray for them, then forgotten? Forgetting to pray is like leaving a wounded fellow soldier behind on the battlefield. I need You to help me remember, Lord, for my mind is easily overrun. I trust You to be my general and bring them to mind when the need is greatest. Help me keep my heart and ears open to Your commands. Amen.

....

....

....

....

Evening
NO WANTS

The LORD is my shepherd; I shall not want.
PSALM 23:1 KJV

Since You are looking out for me—guarding and guiding me—I have everything I need. You are the Good Shepherd who supplies everything to me, Your sheep. Remind me every day that as a sheep, I cannot see the bigger picture—the dangers over the hill or the blessings that are mine to find. Help me more fully trust the Shepherd and His plans for me. Give me a heart of gratitude and a spirit that relinquishes control. Thank You, Lord.

....

....

....

....

Morning

OPEN EYES, ENDLESS HOPE

*I pray that the eyes of your heart may be enlightened, so that you
will know what is the hope of His calling, what are the riches
of the glory of His inheritance in the saints, and what is the
boundless greatness of His power toward us who believe.*

EPHESIANS 1:18–19 NASB

Each morning You open the eyes of my heart and fill me with Your power.
I am filled with endless hope. I revel in Your glorious riches. I am saved by
the power of belief. Enlighten me as we spend these moments together. I
await Your words, dear Lord.

....

....

....

....

....

Evening

EXPERIENCING GOD'S STRENGTH

God is my strength and power, and He makes my way perfect.

2 SAMUEL 22:33 NKJV

Life's demands seem heavier than ever before. I am taking a moment right
now to recharge my soul with Your strength. Remind me that my help
comes from You—whatever I need. You are my power source. Fill me up
physically, mentally, and emotionally. I don't have to go through my life
alone. You are always there to recharge me when my power supply is running
low. I rest in You today.

....

....

....

....

Morning

MORNING PRAYER FOR GODLY WORDS

*The Sovereign Lord has given me his words of wisdom, so
that I know how to comfort the weary. Morning by morning
he wakens me and opens my understanding to his will.*

Isaiah 50:4 NLT

Lord, here I am this morning, awaiting Your words of wisdom. Give me
direction. Open my eyes, heart, and spirit to understanding Your will for
my life. I want to know how to speak words that comfort, direct, and assist.
Help me, O Lord. Guide the words of my tongue.

....

....

....

....

Evening

NONE LIKE YOU

*"No one is holy like the Lord, for there is none
besides You, nor is there any rock like our God."*

1 Samuel 2:2 NKJV

God, when I consider my own inadequacies, I am amazed at Your perfectness. You are truth and justice, holiness and integrity. You are the one true
God. Other deities disappoint their followers; other idols fail. You never
do. Because You are perfect holiness, all Your other attributes are only
good. There is no selfishness, vengefulness, or deceitfulness in You, Lord.
I can trust You completely and revel in Your light unafraid. Amen.

....

....

....

....

....

Morning

RIGHT THERE WITH ME

I will praise the LORD, who counsels me; even at night my heart instructs me.

PSALM 16:7 NIV

Dear God, I have often gone to sleep with a problem weighing on my mind and woken up in the morning with a solution that seemed to appear as I slept. Those miraculous solutions come from You. Thank You, Lord, for counseling me in the night, for instructing me even when I am unaware. It comforts me to know that even when I don't see Your hand or hear Your voice, You are right there with me. Amen.

....

....

....

....

Evening

MADE A MISTAKE

Indeed, we all make many mistakes. For if we could control our tongues, we would be perfect and could also control ourselves in every other way.

JAMES 3:2 NLT

O God, if only I could control my tongue! My life is more like "open mouth, insert foot." And that's just what I've done. Is there any way to remedy this situation? Give me the courage to be humble, to admit I've made a mistake. Help us put this incident behind us. Give me the wisdom to do better next time. All to Your glory!

....

....

....

....

....

Morning
LIKE BIRDS

*Consider the ravens: for they neither sow nor reap; which
neither have storehouse nor barn; and God feedeth them:
how much more are ye better than the fowls?*
LUKE 12:24 KJV

Lord, if You keep track of the lives of birds, then I know I can trust You to watch over my own life. May I rest in the knowledge that You are always looking after me. I know I am worth much more to You than a bird. And even though I know I don't deserve it, I thank You for Your unconditional love.

....

....

....

....

Evening
PRIORITIES

*Therefore I say unto you, Take no thought for your life, what ye shall
eat, or what ye shall drink; nor yet for your body, what ye shall put
on. Is not the life more than meat, and the body than raiment?*
MATTHEW 6:25 KJV

Father, when I start to worry over small things, help me keep my priorities in order. Give me grace not to make mountains out of molehills. Time and time again, You have proven that You are faithful, so why should I worry? Keep my heart steadfast and my footing secure.

....

....

....

....

....

Morning

JESUS' WORD POWER

[Jesus said,] "The Spirit alone gives eternal life. Human effort accomplishes nothing. And the very words I have spoken to you are spirit and life."
JOHN 6:63 NLT

I try and try, but my efforts accomplish nothing when I have not come first to You in prayer. I need to do things in Your strength, for otherwise I am useless. I need Your power behind me when I speak. Allow Your Word to speak to me. Guide my way by Your gentle voice. May my spirit and Yours become one today.

....

....

....

....

....

Evening

LIVING MY FAITH

*If you claim to be religious but don't control your tongue,
you are fooling yourself, and your religion is worthless.*
JAMES 1:26 NLT

Lord, I want to live my faith. To do that I need to control my words, but sometimes my tongue seems to have a mind of its own. Help me rein in my mouth. Give me words that will lead my children to You. Help me live a life that is rich in Your love—and may that love affect my speech. Show me how to live this faith.

....

....

....

....

Morning

THE INSPIRATIONAL WORD

All Scripture is God-breathed and is useful for teaching,
rebuking, correcting and training in righteousness.
2 TIMOTHY 3:16 NIV

Lord, Your Word thrills me, convicts me, comforts me, and strengthens me. Thank You for inspiring the prophets as they penned Your truth. Thank You for protecting the scripture through centuries of skepticism and persecution. Thank You for giving me the blessing of this treasure. When I am hungry, Your Word feeds me; when I am fearful, it assures me; when I am uncertain, it guides me. Your Book is the light upon my path. Without it, I would be lost. Amen.

....

....

....

....

Evening

THREE STEPS TO GOOD SPEECH

Everyone should be quick to listen, slow to speak and slow to become angry.
JAMES 1:19 NIV

Step number one: I need to work on my listening skills. Too often I find myself thinking of a response instead of listening to what people are saying, and then I am rushing in with a comment before they're even finished talking. Help me listen and wait. Step number two: Remind me to pray before I speak. I need to be patient. And step number three: Take away my anger. Calm my spirit.

....

....

....

....

Morning

PRAYER AND THANKSGIVING

*Be careful for nothing; but in every thing by prayer and supplication
with thanksgiving let your requests be made known unto God.*

PHILIPPIANS 4:6 KJV

Even while I'm asking You for something, Lord, I can already thank You.
I know You hear my prayers and will answer with "Yes," "No," or "Wait."
Thank You for often taking care of my needs even before I ask. What a
comfort it is that You already know what I need. I can trust You absolutely
to answer me in the best way and according to Your purpose.

....

....

....

....

....

Evening

SAFE FROM DANGER

*For in the day of trouble he will keep me safe in his dwelling; he will
hide me in the shelter of his sacred tent and set me high upon a rock.*

PSALM 27:5 NIV

Lord, I need Your protection. Keep me safe in Your dwelling place. Hide
me from my enemies in Your secure shelter. Comfort me with Your warm
blanket of peace and love. I am safe with You, and in Your protection—in
Your presence—I can move from fearful to fearless, from timid to trusting.
Here, Lord, I am safe from harm.

....

....

....

....

Morning
DIVERSE GIFTS

There are different kinds of gifts, but the same Spirit.
1 CORINTHIANS 12:4 NIV

Dear God, there are times when I get frustrated with the church—it has its challenges. But so does a human body. And yet when each bodily organ serves its function, there is life and energy. Help me remember that You made my spiritual brothers and sisters with diverse gifts; help me work with, not against, them. Thank You for reminding me again today that this family of God is one of Your treasures, a blessing from Your hand—and heart. Amen.

....

....

....

....

....

Evening
NEVER ALONE

I will never leave you nor forsake you.
JOSHUA 1:5 NIV

Your Word says that You will never leave me, but right now I feel all alone. I am afraid of what lies before me. Help me know, beyond a shadow of a doubt, that You are with me. You are my Good Shepherd. With You by my side, I need not fear. Fill me with Your presence and Your courage as I greet this day.

....

....

....

....

....

Morning
GOD'S EARS

And if we know that he hear us, whatsoever we ask,
we know that we have the petitions that we desired of him.
1 JOHN 5:15 KJV

Thank You, God, that You are always listening to me. You never ignore my prayers, no matter how silly or insignificant I think my words might be. It's a mystery how You can possibly hear the requests of all of mankind at the same time, but You do! And each moment of communication is important to You. Thank You for being a God with always-listening ears.

....

....

....

....

....

Evening
A PRAYER FOR DELIVERANCE

I sought the LORD, and He heard me, and delivered me from all my fears.
PSALM 34:4 NKJV

Lord, I am looking in Your Word for courage and strength. Help me have more confidence in You. I want to commune with You, rest with You, be head over heels "in trust" with You. Show me how to do that, Lord. As I look upon Your face, deliver me from this burden of fear. I want to dwell in Your presence here and now. You are my courage and my strength. Nothing can harm me.

....

....

....

....

Morning
STRONGER

And we know that all things work together for good to them that love God, to them who are the called according to his purpose.
ROMANS 8:28 KJV

Lord, this is a difficult season in my life. I am faced with stresses that I never imagined before. I am amazed at the strength You are giving me daily. Lord, I *know* this is all from You. You are using all these things for Your glory. I know I won't look back from heaven and say anything other than *hallelujah*. I am saying it now. *Hallelujah.*

....

....

....

....

....

Evening
NO DOUBT

But when you ask, you must believe and not doubt, because the one who doubts is like a wave of the sea, blown and tossed by the wind.
JAMES 1:6 NIV

Lord, rescue me from my sea of doubt and fear. I have lived with uncertainty and suspicion for too long. I ask that You would quiet my stormy emotions and help me believe that You will take care of me. When I'm tempted to be cynical, help me choose to step away from fear and closer to faith.

....

....

....

....

....

Morning

NO MAN CAN HARM ME

So we say with confidence, "The Lord is my helper;
I will not be afraid. What can mere mortals do to me?"

HEBREWS 13:6 NIV

I claim this promise for myself today, Lord. You are my helper and I will *not* be afraid of anything! You are my Rock and Refuge. You shield me from any troubles this world can throw at me. I feel Your hands upon mine. Nothing can harm me with You by my side. I arise with confidence, telling the whole world, "The Lord is my helper! I am not afraid!"

....

....

....

....

Evening

PROMISES

Whatsoever we ask, we receive of him, because we keep his
commandments, and do those things that are pleasing in his sight.

1 JOHN 3:22 KJV

Help me keep Your commandments and always live in a way that pleases You, my Lord. I know Your commandments are meant not to be a burden to me but to keep me safe from harm, from temptations, and to allow me to live in the freedom of Your love. Forgive me for the times I feel like Your laws are constraining to me.

....

....

....

....

....

Morning
TO EVERY GENERATION

Your faithfulness endures to all generations.

PSALM 119:90 NKJV

Jehovah God, I come to revel in Your faithfulness. From generations past to this very minute, multitudes have testified that You always come through. Yet there have been times in my life when I thought You had overlooked me, that You didn't hear my prayers. But my doubts proved false, and Your record is untarnished. You didn't promise that I would always understand Your ways, but You did promise Your presence and love in every circumstance. And I can testify it's true. I love You, Lord. Amen.

Evening
LEANING ON THE WORD

For you have been my hope, Sovereign LORD, my confidence since my youth.

PSALM 71:5 NIV

Lord, You have been my hope. You give me confidence to face the day. When I am afraid, all I need to do is remember Your Word and trust in that. Your Word is my confidence and my strength. When misfortunes come my way, help me lean back and rest in Your Word, committing Your promises to memory, strengthening my spirit and my soul.

Morning

PERSISTENCE!

*Ask, and it shall be given you; seek, and ye shall
find; knock, and it shall be opened unto you.*

MATTHEW 7:7 KJV

May I trust You enough, Lord, to ask You for what I need—and then to keep asking, seeking, and knocking, until You answer. Help me never grow weary of coming to You in prayer. I know that You will keep Your promises—that You hear me and are working in the details of my life. When I am praying for others, keep me committed to taking them to You.

....

....

....

....

....

Evening

NO FEAR IN LOVE

*There is no fear in love. But perfect love drives out fear, because fear has
to do with punishment. The one who fears is not made perfect in love.*

1 JOHN 4:18 NIV

Lord, thank You that Your great love conquers fear! I can love people freely because You live in me. I don't have to fear rejection. I may not always be accepted, but either way I can love with confidence because Your perfect love drives out fear. Give me the courage to live that life of love.

....

....

....

....

....

Morning
BRIGHTER

*The unfolding of Your [glorious] words give light; their
unfolding gives understanding to the simple (childlike).*

PSALM 119:130 AMP

Heavenly Father, sometimes it is so dark here. Not just the darkness of night: the darkness of sin and unknowing presses close. I am reaching up for Your light. Thank You, Lord, for Your Word. It comforts and illuminates in a way that nothing else does. It makes You present and real to me. Thank You for giving me something that is so *alive* with Your Spirit to be my anchor and lantern in the darkness. Amen.

....

....

....

....

Evening
GOD STRENGTHENS YOU

*So do not fear, for I am with you; do not be dismayed, for I am your God. I will
strengthen you and help you; I will uphold you with my righteous right hand.*

ISAIAH 41:10 NIV

Lord, I need Your strength. Stronger than steel, your character is so solid I don't have to be afraid. I can have joy because of Your joy in me. With Your righteous right hand You help me, deliver me, and uphold me. As You take my hand and say, *"Do not fear, I will help you,"* I smile in gratitude and thanks.

....

....

....

....

....

Morning
CONFIDENCE

Therefore I say unto you, What things soever ye desire, when ye pray, believe that ye receive them, and ye shall have them.

MARK 11:24 KJV

Thank You, Father, that I can come to You in confidence. I am unworthy to be given access to You through prayer, yet You delight in the communication we have. When I bring requests to You, I want those requests to be things that are not selfish or outside of Your will. Grant that my desires are Your desires, Father. I know that You will always give me whatever I truly need.

....

....

....

....

....

Evening
JOY IN GIVING

Each of you should give what you have decided in your heart to give, not reluctantly or under compulsion, for God loves a cheerful giver.

2 CORINTHIANS 9:7 NIV

Lord, thank You for Your blessings. I want to be a cheerful giver. I desire to give from a full heart that serves, not reluctantly or with complaining. I long to see Your money used in ways that will bless others—through my tithing at church, giving to mission organizations, or helping the needy. I choose to give at whatever level I can—and ask You to bless it.

....

....

....

....

Morning
SEEDLINGS

And he took the children in his arms,
placed his hands on them and blessed them.
MARK 10:16 NIV

Dear Father, I know my children give You as much joy as they give me, and I just want to thank You for them today. Thank You for their quick minds, healthy bodies, loving hearts, and hilarious antics. Most of the time I'm so busy that I don't take even a moment to praise You for what awesome creations they are. Give me grace as I continue to point their hearts to You. Amen.

....

....

....

....

Evening
GOD WILL PROVIDE

"Look at the birds of the air; they do not sow or reap or store away in barns,
and yet your heavenly Father feeds them. Are you not much more valuable
than they? Can any one of you by worrying add a single hour to your life?"
MATTHEW 6:26–27 NIV

Lord, thank You for providing my needs. I give You those nagging thoughts about lacking money for clothes, food, and the basics. You feed the sparrows in the field, Lord—You'll certainly help me and my family. I praise You for Your goodness, Lord, and the faithfulness of Your provision.

....

....

....

....

....

Morning
TOMORROW

*Take therefore no thought for the morrow: for the
morrow shall take thought for the things of itself.*
MATTHEW 6:34 KJV

The truth is that I have no control over tomorrow, Lord. Free me from worries about the future, whether tomorrow or next week or next year. May I rely on You today, so that I can focus on the here and now, this moment, and trust You to take care of whatever comes next. I do trust You, Father. Help my actions be evidence to that fact. I yearn for the freedom that comes from being worry-free!

Evening
THANK YOU FOR MY FRIENDSHIPS

*One who has unreliable friends soon comes to ruin,
but there is a friend who sticks closer than a brother.*
PROVERBS 18:24 NIV

Lord, I thank You for my wonderful friends! I am grateful for the blessings and the joys each one brings to my life. Thank You for my "heart friends," my loyal sister friends who listen, care, and encourage me. They are my faithful companions. I acknowledge that You, Lord, are the giver of all good gifts, and I thank You for Your provision in friendships.

Morning
HEART'S DESIRE

Delight thyself also in the LORD: and he
shall give thee the desires of thine heart.
PSALM 37:4 KJV

Thank You, God, for creating the deepest, truest desires that live within me. You have made me unique from everyone else, and You've given me a desire to live inside Your will. Thank You for the passions and gifts You have given me. Please show me how I can use those gifts to be a blessing to You. I'm glad that as I delight in You, I can trust You always to meet the needs of my yearning heart.

....

....

....

....

Evening
BEING A BETTER LISTENER

Come and hear, all you who fear God; let me tell you what he has done for me.
PSALM 66:16 NIV

Lord, I praise You today for all You have done for me. You have brought help, hope, healing, and restoration! Help me proclaim Your goodness, sharing the amazing ways You have come through for me. As I speak, help me be a good listener too. Through Your spirit, Lord, may I show I care about my friends. Give me wisdom to know when my ears should be open and my mouth shut.

....

....

....

....

....

Morning
THE PAST IS GONE

As far as the east is from the west, so far has
He removed our transgressions from us.

PSALM 103:12 NKJV

Father, I'm glad You have redeemed my past. I've said and done things of which I'm not proud. I'm grateful that You've blotted out my sins and given me a fresh start. Like one using a marker board, You wiped away the shame and guilt and handed the marker back to me. I don't have to live in the past; I can face the future with confidence and grace. In Christ's name, amen.

....

....

....

....

....

Evening
LOVE ONE ANOTHER

[Jesus said], Love one another; as I have loved you.

JOHN 13:34 NKJV

What an example of love You give us, Jesus! You laid down Your life for everyone—even while we were still sinners. Fill me with that kind of love, Lord. I want to be like You, serving others with compassion, understanding, patience, and kindness. Give me that power, that longing, to love those who love me, those who hate me, and those who are indifferent to me.

....

....

....

....

....

Morning
OPEN UP WIDE!

I am the LORD thy God, which brought thee out of the
land of Egypt: open thy mouth wide, and I will fill it.
PSALM 81:10 KJV

Lord, like a baby bird, I will open wide my soul's mouth, knowing that You will always feed me all I need. Open up my heart today, God, and fill it to the brim with just what I need: encouragement, joy, a spirit of servanthood, a passion for the lost, patience, kindness, and a love for others. I'm ready, Father—fill me up!

....

....

....

....

....

Evening
TURNING THE OTHER CHEEK

The LORD also restored the fortunes of Job when he prayed for
his friends, and the LORD increased double all that Job had.
JOB 42:10 NASB

Job prayed for his friends even though they hurt him. When he did this, You blessed him. Sometimes it's hard to overlook the hurtful things people say and do. Help me be more like Job—to learn to turn the other cheek and actually serve friends who disappoint me. I come to You tonight asking for that kind of compassion and dedication to my friends, Lord.

....

....

....

....

Morning
A PERFECT PLACE

Now I saw a new heaven and a new earth, for the
first heaven and the first earth had passed away.
REVELATION 21:1 NKJV

Creator God, I wish there weren't diseases in our world. Although sickness was not present in the Garden of Eden, it is a part of this life now, a consequence of the curse under which our world suffers. But someday You'll create a new earth, and I know bacteria won't stand a chance there. I look forward to that, Father God, for then the world will once again be "very good." Amen.

....

....

....

....

Evening
WAITING ON THE FUTURE

Know also that wisdom is like honey for you: If you find it,
there is a future hope for you, and your hope will not be cut off.
PROVERBS 24:14 NIV

You have made promises to me for my life. I know everything You promised will happen, and I'm excited about the future. Help me find patience to be content doing what I should be doing now while on my way to achieving the purpose You have for my life.

....

....

....

....

....

Morning

SATISFIED

And the LORD shall guide thee continually, and satisfy thy soul in drought, and make fat thy bones: and thou shalt be like a watered garden, and like a spring of water, whose waters fail not.

ISAIAH 58:11 KJV

Even in the midst of life's droughts—when everything seems dry and dead and dusty—thank You, Father, for continuing to water my heart and satisfy my soul. When I see others are in the midst of drought, give me the right words and actions to share Your living water that will keep them from ever being thirsty again.

....

....

....

....

Evening

LOVED NOW AND FOREVER

I am convinced that neither death nor life, neither angels nor demons, neither the present nor the future, nor any powers, neither height nor depth, nor anything else in all creation, will be able to separate us from the love of God that is in Christ Jesus our Lord.

ROMANS 8:38–39 NIV

No matter what happens, Lord, I cannot be separated from You and Your love. Oh, what that means to me! Fill me with the love that never ends. May my life be filled with blessings, and may I praise You every day.

....

....

....

....

....

Morning

HUNGRY SOULS

For he satisfieth the longing soul, and filleth the hungry soul with goodness.
PSALM 107:9 KJV

God, my soul gets so hungry for You sometimes. I know that it's not You who has moved away, but the problem is with me. Thank You that You are immovable, unshakable, and always there. Because of this, I know just where to run to find You, to satisfy my longing soul. Give me a firm footing in Your presence so I am not tempted to wander away again. Thank You for being patient with me.

....

....

....

....

....

Evening

UNKNOWN FUTURE

Indeed, how can people avoid what they don't know is going to happen?
ECCLESIASTES 8:7 NLT

Dear God, I don't know what lies before me. I feel plagued by the what-ifs that tumble through my mind and pierce my confident spirit. Allow me to let You fill my soul. Help me be confident in Your wisdom and power to guide me so that, although You have concealed from me the knowledge of future events, I may be ready for any changes that arise.

....

....

....

....

....

Morning

INTERNAL CLOCKS

*To declare Your lovingkindness in the
morning, and Your faithfulness every night.*

PSALM 92:2 NKJV

Heavenly Father, it seems like every person has an internal rhythm set to a certain time in the day. There are early birds and night owls and middle-of-the-day people. Not many of us are successful in changing our internal clock. Maybe You wanted to create humans with varying peak hours of energy. It would be a pretty boring world if we all fizzled out at the same time each day. Thank You for the variety You have provided in all of us. Amen.

....

....

....

....

Evening

GOD'S PLAN OF BLESSING

*"I am the LORD your God, who teaches you to benefit,
who leads you in the way you should go."*

ISAIAH 48:17 NASB

The Bible tells me that whatever I put my hand to will prosper. I am blessed in the city and in the field, when I come into my house and when I go out of it. Your blessing on my life provides for my every need. I ask for Your wisdom, Lord. Help me make the right choices and decisions for my life. You make me a blessing because I belong to You.

....

....

....

....

....

Morning
ROOTSTOCK

*Know therefore that the LORD your God is God; he is the faithful
God, keeping his covenant of love to a thousand generations
of those who love him and keep his commandments.*

DEUTERONOMY 7:9 NIV

Dear Father, You are a God who is always faithful. Thank You for the men and women in my family tree who loved You and passed a godly heritage down to me. I praise You that You are the same yesterday, today, and tomorrow. And I praise You that my children and their children's children can follow the same unchanging God. Amen.

....

....

....

....

Evening
GOD'S PLANS

*But the plans of the LORD stand firm forever,
the purposes of his heart through all generations.*

PSALM 33:11 NIV

You have led me to this place where I now lie before You, seeking Your presence and Your face, Your guidance and Your strength. Your plans for my life stand firm. With one glance, You see all the generations that have gone before, that are present now, and that will come in the future. Allow me to rest in the knowledge that each day You go before me, and in the end, all will be well with my soul.

....

....

....

....

Morning
RICH IN GRACE

*In whom we have redemption through his blood, the
forgiveness of sins, according to the riches of his grace.*
EPHESIANS 1:7 KJV

The world tells me I should be rich in material wealth, Father, but true riches are found in Your limitless grace. Thank You for the richness of Your grace, Lord. Thank You that Your grace is large enough to cover all my past sin, my current sin, and my future sin. That's the kind of rich inheritance I truly desire!

....

....

....

....

....

Evening
FOR GOOD HEALTH

*"Say to him: 'Long life to you! Good health to you and
your household! And good health to all that is yours!'"*
1 SAMUEL 25:6 NIV

Lord, thank You for my good health. I pray for Your power to sustain me as I take care of myself—by eating healthy food, drinking enough water, and making movement and exercise a part of my daily life. Give me the self-control and motivation I need to make wise choices to support my health. Please keep me from injury and illness, and keep me safe.

....

....

....

....

Morning
WATERED

*He dawns on them like the morning light when the sun
rises on a cloudless morning, when the tender grass springs
out of the earth through clear shining after rain.*

2 SAMUEL 23:4 AMPC

Dear Father, I thank You for things that remind me to lift my arms in praise. When I praise You, Lord, I feel so different: washed clean with joy. I feel like a plant after a spring rain. I praise You for the beauty of the earth, the skies, and the heavens, and for Your great love, which surrounds and sustains it all. Amen.

....

....

....

....

Evening
GETTING RID OF STRESS

Cast all your anxiety on him because he cares for you.

1 PETER 5:7 NIV

Lord, help me find relief from stress. I need to value rest and make time to relax—and I need Your power to do so. I cast my cares on You. Help me deal with the toxic, unhealthy relationships in my life. Give me the strength to say no when I need better emotional boundaries. And please help me find joy again in the things I enjoy doing. Calm me and renew me, Lord.

....

....

....

....

....

Morning
PROMISES

*This is my blood of the new testament,
which is shed for many for the remission of sins.*
MATTHEW 26:28 KJV

Jesus' blood is the new testament—the new promise You have made to me, Lord. I am not bound by the rules and regulations of the Old Testament law, but instead I have been given amazing freedom! The blood of Jesus is so powerful that I cannot comprehend it, but please help me rely on His saving blood that heals all my sins always.

Evening
WHEN HEALING DOES NOT COME

*I consider that our present sufferings are not worth
comparing with the glory that will be revealed in us.*
ROMANS 8:18 NIV

Lord, it's hard to know why You don't heal when You clearly have the power to do so. Help me resist focusing on my present suffering and be transformed in my attitude. May I revel in the glory that will be revealed in me through this. I don't understand, but I choose to praise You anyway. Give me the peace, comfort, and assurance that all things, even this, will work for my good and for Your glory.

Morning

FITNESS

"Physical training is good, but training for godliness is much better, promising benefits in this life and in the life to come."
1 TIMOTHY 4:8 NLT

It's an exercise-crazy world we live in, Lord. Some people make this area of self-care too important; they spend an inordinate amount of time on it. Yet others don't keep it high enough on their priority list. Help me, God, to keep the proper perspective of fitness, because, after all, I have a responsibility for the upkeep on this body. It's on loan from You. Amen.

....

....

....

....

Evening

UNDER CONTROL

"The LORD is slow to anger, abounding in love and forgiving sin and rebellion. Yet he does not leave the guilty unpunished; he punishes the children for the sin of the parents to the third and fourth generation."
NUMBERS 14:18 NIV

Overwhelming hurt makes it easy to be angry, Lord. We have less patience with others, situations become stressful, and it's hard to keep life under control. Remind me of Your own nature, which forgave me for so much. You call me not to accept quick anger but to avoid all wrongdoing that deserves punishment.

....

....

....

....

....

Morning
FAITHFUL

If we confess our sins, he is faithful and just to forgive
us our sins, and to cleanse us from all unrighteousness.
1 JOHN 1:9 KJV

God, I confess to You that I have sinned. I have gone astray from Your love.
Again and again I fall short. It shames me to admit it, but You ask for my
confession. Forgive me. Bring me home. Thank You that even now, I can
rely on Your faithful love. Thank You for the promise that You are faithful
to forgive me—not just yesterday and today, but tomorrow as well.

....

....

....

....

Evening
GOD AS LORD

Yes, happy (blessed, fortunate, prosperous, to be
envied) are the people whose God is the Lord!
PSALM 144:15 AMPC

Just knowing You, Lord, is my greatest blessing. When I rest in You, I am
in the right place. Joy, security, and love come from Your hand, and nothing
I could buy fills the empty places of my heart as Your Spirit does. Thank
You for every blessing You have granted me. Since You care about all of
my life, I live securely. Nothing lies beyond Your plan and power. I want
to remember that every second.

....

....

....

....

....

Morning
COMFORT

"Blessed are those who mourn, for they shall be comforted."
MATTHEW 5:4 NKJV

Lord, I know if I never experienced sorrow, I'd also never feel the comfort that surpasses all this earth can offer. Your love reaches places inside me no human affection can touch. When I'm deeply hurt, Your Spirit consoles me in powerful, unexpected ways. When I mourn, I know You stand right with me in the pain. Thank You for healing my heart and giving me relief I can share with others. You alone give perfect peace to the human heart. Thank You, Jesus.

....

....

....

....

Evening
STAKED

The eternal God is your refuge and dwelling place,
and underneath are the everlasting arms.
DEUTERONOMY 33:27 AMPC

Lord, the wind is howling like a beast around the house tonight. Everything that is not nailed down tight rattles and moans. Sometimes, Lord, when the wind howls so and reminds me of my frailty, I wonder how long *I* can hold on. How many more tragedies, trials, and temptations? But then You are there, beloved Savior, reminding me of the everlasting arms that are always around me, comforting, sustaining, and protecting. Thank You, Jesus. I stake my life on You. Amen.

....

....

....

Morning
POWER

The Son of man hath power on earth to forgive sins.
MARK 2:10 KJV

Jesus, no one else has the power to forgive sins like You do. You took the shame of my sins on Your shoulders as You hung on the cross. I cannot understand the immense pain and suffering You endured as You were beaten and ridiculed. You paid for me. You took care of my insurmountable debt. Thank You for Your sacrifice, and thank You for Your power that sets me free from my sins.

....
....
....
....

Evening
STRENGTH IN GOD

Then you will have success if you are careful to observe the decrees and laws that the LORD gave Moses for Israel. Be strong and courageous. Do not be afraid or discouraged.
1 CHRONICLES 22:13 NIV

With You by my side, I can fend off fear and expect success. When I believe that You hold my future and allow Your Word to be my guide, strength and courage will be mine. Help me cling faithfully to Your Word, Lord. I want to be in the place where You can bless me. May Your courage empower me.

....
....
....
....
....

Morning
SLICE OF LIFE

Make the most of every opportunity in these evil days.
EPHESIANS 5:16 NLT

Dear Lord, the transition of minutes to hours is so incremental that it is tedious to observe. It's much easier to focus on a large chunk of time than a myriad of tiny ones. Yet hours are made up of minutes, just like the body is comprised of cells. Each is vital to the whole. Lord, help me remember that each minute of the day is a small section, a slice of my life. Help me make the best use of every minute. Amen.

....

....

....

....

Evening
REAL PROSPERITY

"Hear me, O Judah and you inhabitants of Jerusalem:
Believe in the LORD your God, and you shall be
established; believe His prophets, and you shall prosper."
2 CHRONICLES 20:20 NKJV

Faith and blessing cannot be separated. Thank You for all the good things You have given me. Even in times of trial, don't let me become ungrateful. But more than that, remind me of the spiritual blessings You've offered me day by day. Without You I could never know true peace of mind and heart or experience Your deep love. Thank You, Jesus, for all these blessings.

....

....

....

....

....

Morning

GOD'S NAME

Help us, O God of our salvation, for the glory of thy name:
and deliver us, and purge away our sins, for thy name's sake.

PSALM 79:9 KJV

I know that my sins make me dirty, God. More than that, my sins separate me from You. But because You are who You are, You make me clean, Lord. You cover me in the blood of the Lamb, and You deliver me from all my sin so that I may dwell in Your presence. It's nothing that I've done on my own. May I always bring Your name glory!

....

....

....

....

Evening

MEETING IN JESUS

"I give them eternal life, and they shall never
perish; no one will snatch them out of my hand."

JOHN 10:28 NIV

Lord, I know those who accept Your love cannot die eternally, though death comes to their bodies. I am glad You offered my loved one life forever. I have no control over death, but You hold my loved one safely in Your hand. Though separated now, we will meet again. Together we will worship You forever. Thank You, Jesus. That's just the security I need today.

....

....

....

....

....

Morning
A JOB FOR ME

"But seek first the kingdom of God and His righteousness,
and all these things shall be added to you."

MATTHEW 6:33 NKJV

Dear heavenly Father, I need a job. There are so many people looking for work; employers have a large pool from which to draw. Still, You've promised to supply my basic needs if I would keep Your kingdom top priority in my life. So I ask that You would direct my search and help me approach this transition with integrity and consideration for my present employer. I ask this in Your name, amen.

....

....

....

....

Evening
SPECK OF FAITH

"If you have faith as a mustard seed, you can say to this mulberry tree, 'Be
pulled up by the roots and be planted in the sea,' and it would obey you."

LUKE 17:6 NKJV

Thank You, Jesus, for the amazing things that happen when I exhibit faith. It takes just a tiny bit to start wonderful things. When even a speck of faith seems hard to come by, Lord, remind me of Your love. I need only ask for help, and You will be with me in a moment. Thank You for Your blessings, Jesus.

....

....

....

....

....

Morning

PURGED

Iniquities prevail against me: as for our
transgressions, thou shalt purge them away.
PSALM 65:3 KJV

I mess up a lot, Father. In fact, sin seems stronger than me sometimes, dear Lord. It takes such a steady foothold in my life that I feel powerless to change. Purge away this tendency from my heart, I pray. I will focus on You and Your Word, Savior God, and I know that You will lead me away from the temptation of sin.

....

....

....

....

....

Evening

GOD'S FAMILY

"Whoever does God's will is my brother and sister and mother."
MARK 3:35 NIV

Actions tell more than any words. Just as I don't want to harm my family name by doing wrong, I desire to lift up Your name, even in trials. No one should blame You for my wrong actions. When I find it hard to keep up the "family name," remind me I have an older brother who provides for me in all things. Thank You, Jesus, for loving me enough to make me part of Your family. I want to honor Your name.

....

....

....

....

Morning
BACKSLIDING

O Lord, though our iniquities testify against us, do thou it for thy name's sake:
for our backslidings are many; we have sinned against thee. . . . Thou,
O Lord, art in the midst of us, and we are called by thy name; leave us not.

JEREMIAH 14:7, 9 KJV

No matter how far along I go in my spiritual walk with You, Lord, I always start to slide backward. There are some temptations that will always make me struggle, and sometimes I succumb to those temptations. And yet You are here with me. Don't leave me now.

....

....

....

....

....

Evening
HEAVENLY FATHER

"No, the Father himself loves you because you have
loved me and have believed that I came from God."

JOHN 16:27 NIV

No matter the state of my earthly family, You remain my eternal Father. When a parent fails me or leaves this earth, I am not left adrift. You still love me, direct me, and guide my steps. I'm so glad I'm part of Your family. Though my love is infinitely less perfect than Yours, my feeble response is enough for You. You pour out love on me because I've accepted Jesus. Thank You for Your love.

....

....

....

....

Morning

GARDENING

For the Son of man is come to seek and to save that which was lost.

LUKE 19:10 KJV

Dear Lord, You are a God who is not afraid of messes. You are not afraid to reach into the tangles and the mire. You see into the future of a lost person's heart: You see a garden where I only see a dangerous wilderness where *I* might get hurt. Lord, I want to be like You; I want to love the lost like You do. Help me look past the mess to the eternal soul inside. Amen.

....

....

....

....

....

....

Evening

FEARLESSNESS IN GOD

The LORD is for me, so I will have no fear. What can mere people do to me? Yes, the LORD is for me; he will help me.

PSALM 118:6–7 NLT

What do I have to fear when You are on my side, Lord? When I'm focused on You, I trust fully in Your power. Help me keep my eyes on You, even when life attempts to get in the way. Turn my heart to Your truths, no matter what this world throws at me. I love and trust You, Lord.

....

....

....

....

....

Morning
GETTING STARTED

The way of the sluggard is blocked with thorns.
PROVERBS 15:19 NIV

Dear Lord, the first step toward any goal is the hardest, and I don't feel motivated to take it. Procrastination is a terrible hindrance. I know. I'm a procrastinator. I don't like to admit it, but You see it anyway. Thank You for giving me more chances than I deserve. Remind me that I just need to start. Inspiration often springs from soil watered with obedience. Let me learn this lesson well. Amen.

....

....

....

....

Evening
STRONG PEACE

The LORD will give strength to His people;
the LORD will bless His people with peace.
PSALM 29:11 NKJV

Your peace is my strength, Lord. When Your serenity fills my heart, I easily head in Your direction. I know whom I serve and where I need to go. Together we walk in the eternal way. Thank You, Jesus, for promising me Your peace. Your blessing is larger than any predicament. I need Your peace. May Your Spirit pour it out on my life so I can pass Your strength on to others.

....

....

....

....

....

Morning

REBELLION

*To the Lord our God belong mercies and
forgivenesses, though we have rebelled against him.*
DANIEL 9:9 KJV

Sometimes I act like a child—I want to do what I want to do when I want to do it. I disregard what I know is right and good and travel down a dangerous path. Even when I'm in the middle of the situation, I know I'm doing wrong. I rebel against Your love, Lord. Thank You for always forgiving me, even though I don't deserve it. Help me never take advantage of Your forgiveness.

....

....

....

....

Evening

SEEK CHRIST NOW

Seek ye the LORD while he may be found, call ye upon him while he is near.
ISAIAH 55:6 KJV

How You long to save the lost and dying, Lord Jesus! How eager You are to cleanse us from our sins. From the sweet voices of tiny children to the final breaths of elderly grandparents, the plea for forgiveness and salvation fills You with delight. O Father, may many more people seek You while You may be found.

....

....

....

....

....

Morning
EMPLOYER WOES

*Whatever you do, work at it with all your heart,
as working for the Lord, not for human masters.*
COLOSSIANS 3:23 NIV

God, I have the most demanding boss ever. I need to demonstrate the love of Christ, but it can be challenging when my superior is so hard to please. Give me courage, Lord, to rise above my emotions. Help me pray for my boss and serve as though my assignments come from You. You, Lord, are my true superior. Bless my boss today, God, and show Your love to him through me. Amen.

....

....

....

....

Evening
IN A LOOKING GLASS

*But we all, with open face beholding as in a glass the
glory of the Lord, are changed into the same image
from glory to glory, even as by the Spirit of the Lord.*
2 CORINTHIANS 3:18 KJV

The more I seek You, Lord, the more I become like You. It's a work You began when You agreed to go to the cross for my sins. To be identified with You is the utmost privilege. Oh, what a glorious day is coming when I become like You, for I will see You as You are!

....

....

....

....

....

Morning

MERCIFUL

I will be merciful to their unrighteousness, and their
sins and their iniquities will I remember no more.
HEBREWS 8:12 KJV

Thank You that You are a merciful God. You don't even remember all the many times I let You down! You truly forgive and forget. Teach me how to show this kind of mercy to people in my life who have wronged me—that I may shine Your light to others in a real and genuine way, with unconditional love.

....

....

....

....

Evening

WORK IT OUT

Wherefore, my beloved, as ye have always obeyed, not as
in my presence only, but now much more in my absence,
work out your own salvation with fear and trembling.
PHILIPPIANS 2:12 KJV

Almighty God, Your salvation ensures I will spend eternity with You, but it means so much more than that. I am saved to bring glory to Your name and enjoy Your presence. You have a plan for me now that You've given this marvelous gift. I must honor and live for You. I must bring others to You.

....

....

....

....

....

Morning
DIFFICULT PEOPLE

*Bear with each other and forgive one another
if any of you has a grievance against someone.*
COLOSSIANS 3:13 NIV

Dear Lord, I ask You to help me be patient and kind today. That's what I need as I deal with difficult people and irritating situations. I know there will be people today who will irk me. In those moments when I want to scream, help me remember to forbear and forgive. It's just so easy to react, but help me instead deliberately choose my response. I'm depending on Your power, Father. Amen.

....

....

....

....

....

Evening
PERFECTION

*As for God, his way is perfect; the word of the LORD
is tried: he is a buckler to all them that trust in him.*
2 SAMUEL 22:31 KJV

Your way is perfect, Lord. You will never steer me wrong. When I face confusion, I wonder what my next step should be, but Your Word guides me. It answers my questions about life, tells me how to handle relationships, instructs me in my role as a child of God, and encourages me daily. You have truly given me all I need to succeed.

....

....

....

....

Morning
DELIGHTED IN MERCY

*Who is a God like unto thee, that pardoneth iniquity, and passeth
by the transgression of the remnant of his heritage? he retaineth
not his anger for ever, because he delighteth in mercy.*

MICAH 7:18 KJV

Father, sometimes when I seek Your forgiveness for a sin that I commit over
and over again, I assume that while You are still forgiving me, You might
be doing so begrudgingly. But the truth is that You delight in mercy! So
You delight in forgiving me? What an amazing thought! What would I
do without Your mercy?

Evening
MEDITATION

*This book of the law shall not depart out of thy mouth; but thou
shalt meditate therein day and night, that thou mayest observe
to do according to all that is written therein: for then thou shalt
make thy way prosperous, and then thou shalt have good success.*

JOSHUA 1:8 KJV

So many things demand my attention, Jesus. I want to do a good job
fulfilling my responsibilities, and I'm grateful You've given me the Bible as
my guidebook. As I pore over each passage, it becomes more obvious that
You want to help me succeed.

Morning

BIRDSONG

*"The LORD your God in your midst, the Mighty One, will
save; He will rejoice over you with gladness, He will quiet you
with His love, He will rejoice over you with singing."*

ZEPHANIAH 3:17 NKJV

Lord, I praise You for the little birds in my garden. They are like sequins on a glorious world! You've thought of everything, Lord, and You rejoice in it. Help me remember that as much as I rejoice in songbirds, You rejoice in me even more. Because I am of more value than many sparrows. But thank You for the sparrows too. Amen.

....

....

....

....

Evening

GROWING DAILY

*As newborn babes, desire the sincere milk
of the word, that ye may grow thereby.*

1 PETER 2:2 KJV

In the spring when new lambs or cows are born, it is fun to watch them eagerly nurse from their mother. How instinctive and wonderful! Father, let me desire Your Word just as these young ones delight in that milk. Let it nourish and sustain me and bring continued growth.

....

....

....

....

....

Morning
BLOTTED OUT

I, even I, am he that blotteth out thy transgressions
for mine own sake, and will not remember thy sins.
ISAIAH 43:25 KJV

God, I'm so thankful that You don't hold grudges. I give You thanks and praise, dear Lord, for You have not only wiped away all my sins but You also don't even remember them! You wipe my slate clean; You give me a new start; You hit the RESET button. You have made me truly free from the past.

....

....

....

....

....

Evening
I WILL REJOICE

And ye now therefore have sorrow: but I will see you again,
and your heart shall rejoice, and your joy no man taketh from you.
JOHN 16:22 KJV

You are with me, dear Jesus. What more could I want? Just being with You makes my heart sing, and it's a joy no one can steal from me. I cherish this treasure, and I want those around me to experience it too. Let my life so exude Your joy that everyone I meet will desire You too.

....

....

....

....

....

....

Morning

INSURMOUNTABLE DISTANCE

*As far as the east is from the west, so far hath
he removed our transgressions from us.*

PSALM 103:12 KJV

Whenever I feel that I'm a hopeless case, that I'll never be able to rise above the sin that I fall into, remind me, Father, that from Your perspective my soul and my sin might as well be in different dimensions, separated by an insurmountable distance. Take away my shame and guilt that I feel about my past sins, and help me rest in the fact that I am completely forgiven.

....

....

....

....

....

Evening

PERFECT PEACE

*Thou wilt keep him in perfect peace, whose mind
is stayed on thee: because he trusteth in thee.*

ISAIAH 26:3 KJV

Such a promise and a challenge are packed into this nugget of scripture. You want us to fill our souls with peace in spite of the terrors around us. If our focus is on You and Your omnipotence, we will trust You. You can envelop us in Your peace. What an amazing God You are!

....

....

....

....

....

Morning

GOOGOLPLEX

He telleth the number of the stars; he calleth them all by their names.
Great is our Lord, and of great power: his understanding is infinite.

PSALM 147:4–5 KJV

Lord, You are infinite and beyond comprehension. I try to think about You in this way, but my mind keeps trying to reduce You to something smaller, something I can wrap my understanding around. I praise You that You are wholly infinite and infinitely holy. Who is like You? I don't understand, but I rest, a speck in Your loving hand. Amen.

....

....

....

....

....

Evening

UNTROUBLED

"Peace I leave with you; my peace I give you. I do not give to you as the
world gives. Do not let your hearts be troubled and do not be afraid."

JOHN 14:27 NIV

Knowing and following You daily is nothing like living in the world, Lord. Anxiety fills the earth as people worry about their futures. The search for rest never ends. But in Your kingdom, You give deep, restful serenity that brings me through the most difficult situation. Turn my heart to trust in You so peace descends upon my soul.

....

....

....

....

Morning

BEHIND GOD'S BACK

Thou hast in love to my soul delivered it from the pit of corruption: for thou hast cast all my sins behind thy back.

ISAIAH 38:17 KJV

I have to imagine that if You put something behind Your back, Creator God, it doesn't really even exist anymore. You don't want to look at it, think about it, or even be bothered by it. Always remind me that this is what You have done with my sins! I am free!

....

....

....

....

....

Evening

JOY IN SORROW

Light shines on the righteous and joy on the upright in heart. Rejoice in the LORD, you who are righteous, and praise his holy name.

PSALM 97:11–12 NIV

I may not feel joyful right now, Lord, but I trust Your promise will be fulfilled. Because today doesn't feel wonderful doesn't mean You have forgotten me. Your light still guides me and leads me. Thank You for Your faithfulness to me, Lord, no matter what I experience. I praise You for being there, willing to help me, no matter what I face.

....

....

....

....

....

Morning

SATISFIED

The poor will eat and be satisfied; those who seek the
LORD will praise him—may your hearts live forever!
PSALM 22:26 NIV

Though I've experienced Your saving grace, my heart sometimes still feels empty, Jesus. If my heart echoes with doubt, it's because I have not turned in trust to You. I want to be satisfied with the blessings You've prepared for me, Lord, and share them with others too. Daily turn my heart to Your truths, and help me speak Your praises to the world.

....
....
....
....

Evening

GRACE IN THE NOT-KNOWING

So when. . .this mortal shall have put on immortality, then shall be brought
to pass the saying that is written, Death is swallowed up in victory.
1 CORINTHIANS 15:54 KJV

Lord, tonight I've cried and cried, and You've listened and loved me and given me words of truth and comfort. Someone I love is with You tonight. I don't know how to rejoice that she is walking on streets of gold and at the same time weep that her children will grow up without her. Please help me live with grace in the not-knowing. Amen.

....
....
....
....
....

Morning
UNLIMITED RESOURCES

"For every animal of the forest is mine, and the cattle on a thousand hills."
PSALM 50:10 NIV

Father, You have unlimited resources. So I'm asking You to supply a special need I have today. Although I try to be a good steward of the money You give me, some unexpected event has caught me without the necessary funds. I know You can remedy this situation, if You deem that good for me. Because You're my Father, I'm asking for Your financial advice. I need Your wisdom in this area of my life. Amen.

....

....

....

....

Evening
THE PEACE OF GOD'S CHILDREN

And all thy children shall be taught of the LORD;
and great shall be the peace of thy children.
ISAIAH 54:13 KJV

There is no teacher greater than You, Lord. When we learn from You, we discover all we need to know about the world and the people around us. We have no reason to fear, for we have received our instruction from the Master. I dedicate myself to helping those I love discover the lessons You have for them so they can be at peace.

....

....

....

....

....

Morning

THE DEPTHS OF THE SEA

He will have compassion upon us; he will subdue our iniquities;
and thou wilt cast all their sins into the depths of the sea.
MICAH 7:19 KJV

Thank You for Your loving compassion, heavenly Father, that throws my sin to the bottom of the darkest, deepest ocean—never to be thought of again. Take all the selfish urges of my heart and subdue them so that I may be free to serve You as I long to.

....

....

....

....

....

Evening

STRENGTH AND PEACE

The LORD will give strength unto his people;
the LORD will bless his people with peace.
PSALM 29:11 KJV

It's interesting the way You couple strength and peace. It almost seems as if they don't go together. Still, I am reminded of a father as he plays with his children. He's strong and could easily hurt them, but he loves them and keeps his strength under control. They feel safe and loved and at peace. That's how we feel in Your presence, Lord.

....

....

....

....

....

Morning
NEW CLOTHES

*Take away the filthy garments from him. And unto him
he said, Behold, I have caused thine iniquity to pass from
thee, and I will clothe thee with change of raiment.*

ZECHARIAH 3:4 KJV

Lord, You offer me a brand-new wardrobe to replace my filthy clothes that
are stained with sin. Forgive me when I wrongfully believe that my dirty
rags are adequate and I try to hold on to them. Help me put on the new
clothes You hold out to me. Dress me in Your love and forgiveness.

....

....

....

....

....

Evening
CREATED FOR A PURPOSE

*For by him were all things created, that are in heaven, and that are in
earth, visible and invisible, whether they be thrones, or dominions, or
principalities, or powers: all things were created by him, and for him.*

COLOSSIANS 1:16 KJV

When You spoke this world into existence, when You formed me with Your
hands, they weren't just random acts of Your power. All creation, including
me, is intended to glorify and praise You. I need to convey this message
to those with whom I brush shoulders. Together we can exalt Your name.

....

....

....

....

Morning
COMMUNICATION

I will set nothing wicked before my eyes.
PSALM 101:3 NKJV

Dear God, the internet is a marvelous tool! But the internet also has a great potential for evil. I ask You to protect my family from sites that would have a negative influence on our relationship with You. Help me be prudent in my use of the web. Like any other means of communication, it can be used wrongly. But, with Your help, it can be an instrument for good in our home. Amen.

....

....

....

....

Evening
A SHINING LIGHT

That ye may be blameless and harmless, the sons of God, without rebuke, in the midst of a crooked and perverse nation, among whom ye shine as lights in the world.
PHILIPPIANS 2:15 KJV

Light makes me feel good, Father. I love it when the sun streams through my windows. When the day ends, I'm glad to be able to turn on the lights and brighten my home. Light offers hope. That's what I want to do. I want my friends and neighbors and even people I don't know to see You in me. Let me be a light for You, Father.

....

....

....

....

....

Morning

SHOWERED

Then will I sprinkle clean water upon you, and ye shall be clean:
from all your filthiness, and from all your idols, will I cleanse you.
 EZEKIEL 36:25 KJV

Each time I take a shower, God, remind me that You have showered my soul with Your love. As I lather up with soap that will cleanse the dirt of the day, remind me of the cleansing power of Your grace and mercy. You have washed away everything in me that was false, and now I am truly clean.

....

....

....

....

....

....

Evening

THE JOY OF THE LORD IS MY STRENGTH

For the joy of the LORD is your strength.
NEHEMIAH 8:10 KJV

I'm tired today, dear God. There have been moments when I thought I couldn't take another step. The truth is that I can't move forward without You. But You are with me. Your yoke is easy; Your burden is light. You want to take the pressure off me. What a joy it is for me to walk with You—to draw strength from You. What a wondrous gift to be in Your company.

....

....

....

....

....

Morning
GREAT LOVE

*For great is his love toward us, and the faithfulness
of the LORD endures forever. Praise the LORD.*
PSALM 117:2 NIV

I have a lot to praise You for, Lord. One sorrowful event can't close the door on all You've done for me in the past and Your continued provision for me. As I share my pain with You, Your loving Spirit fills me with comfort. I praise You for the love and faithfulness You've poured out in my life. Thank You, Jesus.

....

....

....

....

....

Evening
CROCUSES

*For the LORD thy God bringeth thee into a good land, a land of brooks
of water, of fountains and depths that spring out of valleys and hills.*
DEUTERONOMY 8:7 KJV

Dear Lord, I praise You for the surprising ways You love us. Thank You for the way rain droplets spangle a branch like diamonds. Thank You for the pictures You paint with sunsets. Thank You for the bright heads of crocuses that spring out of the dregs of winter. Thank You for how You delight in surprising me with the beauty of Your Word and Your world. Amen.

....

....

....

....

Morning
WHENEVER I PRAY

And when ye stand praying, forgive, if ye have ought against any:
that your Father also which is in heaven may forgive you your trespasses.
MARK 11:25 KJV

Whenever I come to You, Lord, asking You to grant me some request, remind me first to let go of any unforgiveness I'm holding in my heart. I don't want to be a grudge holder, and I know that withholding forgiveness hurts me more than it hurts the other person. Show me ways to show true grace—Your grace—to others who have hurt me.

....

....

....

....

....

Evening
IN THE RIGHT DIRECTION

He guides the humble in what is right and teaches them his way.
PSALM 25:9 NIV

When I come to Your side, willing to listen to Your counsel, You set me on the glory road. I can't imagine living without Your guidance. So many blessings come from living for You that I wouldn't want any other lifestyle. Please show me all I need to know today, and lead me in the right way. I don't want to set foot on any path but Yours, Jesus.

....

....

....

....

....

Morning
BEING A PERSON OF ACTION

In the same way, faith by itself, if it is not accompanied by action, is dead.
JAMES 2:17 NIV

Lord, I want to be a person of action—a person of true faith. Faith has to be accompanied by my deeds, Lord. I pray for the wisdom to know when to take risks, when to act, and when to wait. Help me know the right thing to do and the best time to do it. Put true faith into me, Lord, so I can perform the good works You have for me to accomplish.

....

....

....

....

....

Evening
THE TERRIBLE MERCY

"Though he slay me, yet will I hope in him."
JOB 13:15 NIV

Dear Lord, tonight as the sunset faded, the horror of this world seemed to hit me along with the darkness. There are crocuses and raindrops and smiles, but there are also broken marriages and wars and widows. It's so hard to know what to do with all this beauty so inextricably mixed up with all this viciousness. I am crying out to You. Help me trust Your love even as I try to understand it, Lord. Amen.

....

....

....

....

....

Morning
A SHINING LIGHT

*"Let your light so shine before men, that they may see
your good works and glorify your Father in heaven."*
MATTHEW 5:16 NKJV

Dear God, I want to be a better witness for You. Every day I interact with people who aren't believers. Lord, I want to let my light shine before them. I ask You to open up the doors for me today. Let me sense Your prompting. And let the silent witness of my life also speak to others about Your great plan of salvation. In Jesus' name, amen.

....

....

....

....

Evening
MY TESTIMONY

*Having your conversation honest among the Gentiles: that, whereas
they speak against you as evildoers, they may by your good works,
which they shall behold, glorify God in the day of visitation.*
1 PETER 2:12 KJV

Father, by Your grace You saved me. Salvation is a grand gift, and You want me to share it. Some might look for evidence in my life to discredit all I say. Help me live in such a way that they won't find anything. My purpose is to draw them to You. Let my life and speech do just that.

....

....

....

....

....

Morning
ANGER DEFERRED

The discretion of a man deferreth his anger;
and it is his glory to pass over a transgression.
PROVERBS 19:11 KJV

The word *glory* refers to the essence of something, the quality that makes it give forth light. Dear God, remind me that I am most truly myself, my best and shiniest self, when I don't act on my anger against others. Give me the wisdom to know how to react to people and situations in the same way You would react. Let love, respect, and kindness be at the root of everything I do.

....

....

....

....

Evening
GREAT RICHES

There is that maketh himself rich, yet hath nothing:
there is that maketh himself poor, yet hath great riches.
PROVERBS 13:7 KJV

Lord, sometimes I begin thinking about how much easier life would be if I just made more money. Then I consider what that would involve. There would be less time for my family. I'd rarely do the things I really love because I would be busy at work. As I look at it that way, I realize what wonderful riches I have.

....

....

....

....

....

Morning
HOLES

He also brought me up out of a horrible pit. . . .
He has put a new song in my mouth— praise to our God;
many will see it and fear, and will trust in the LORD.

PSALM 40:2–3 NKJV

Dear Lord, when You found me, all I wanted to do was pull the dirt down on my own head and die. But You didn't let me. And You didn't just reach down to me; You jumped *in.* Thank You for changing the ending of my story, Lord. Thank You for the transformative power of Your love. Amen.

....

....

....

....

....

Evening
SOWING AND REAPING

But this I say, He which soweth sparingly shall reap also sparingly;
and he which soweth bountifully shall reap also bountifully.

2 CORINTHIANS 9:6 KJV

You know how much I enjoy my garden, Lord. From the smell of freshly tilled soil to the first seedlings and the earliest harvest, each moment is a reward in its own right. How exciting too to see missionaries on the field, kids saved through children's ministries, and outreach programs begun. As we abundantly sow our garden, let us also abundantly sow seeds for Your harvest.

....

....

....

....

Morning
PERSECUTION

Do good to them that hate you, and pray for them
which despitefully use you, and persecute you.
MATTHEW 5:44 KJV

Father, bless all those who have hurt me, all those who have hurt those I love, all those who have hurt the innocents of our world. I ask that You show me how to reach out my hands in kind and practical ways to these individuals who have brought hurt into our world. Help me see past their actions to their own hurt. Use me to show them Your mercy and love.

....

....

....

....

Evening
SPIRITUAL COURAGE

"Be strong and very courageous. Be careful to obey all the law
my servant Moses gave you; do not turn from it to the right
or to the left, that you may be successful wherever you go."
JOSHUA 1:7 NIV

When I'm trusting in Your promises to me, I cannot go wrong, Lord. It's only when I turn aside from Your guidance that I fall into trouble. Help me stay on track with You. Help me live to do Your will and feel Your peace. Thank You for giving me courage. I don't know how I'd manage without You, Lord.

....

....

....

....

....

DAY 165

Morning

BLESSINGS INSTEAD OF CURSES

Bless them that curse you, and pray for them which despitefully use you.
LUKE 6:28 KJV

My Lord, I feel misused. I feel cursed. I feel slighted and abused. I'm angry and hurt. I come to You with these feelings, and I give them to You. Take away the hurt and my desire for revenge. Give me Your heart when it comes to others. I pray that You would bless the people who have made me feel this way. Your will be done, Father.

Evening

BE CONTENT

Let your conversation be without covetousness; and be content with such things as ye have: for he hath said, I will never leave thee, nor forsake thee.
HEBREWS 13:5 KJV

Lord, I am often tempted to complain. Little things discourage me. I see the gifts that others have received from You and wonder why You haven't given them to me. But then I remember that You are a gift and You've given me far more than I deserve. Help me be content.

Morning
WARMING MY HANDS BY HOLY FIRE

For our God is a consuming fire.
HEBREWS 12:29 NKJV

Dear Lord, it's so cold this morning. My fingers are cold too, but I thank You for a warm cup of tea and a working furnace. You always provide for me and protect me, Lord. Thank You that Your love doesn't wax and wane like the warmth of the sun through the seasons. You are a constant and faithful source of light and warmth for my soul. Don't let me grow cold, Lord, but keep my hands pressed up against Your blaze. Amen.

....

....

....

....

....

Evening
FAITHFUL STUDENT

The advantage of knowledge is this:
that wisdom preserves the life of its possessor.
ECCLESIASTES 7:12 NIV

Lord, I can choose to have a Bible in unread, pristine condition but a life in shambles. Or I can have a used, frayed Bible but a life well ordered by You. Lord, the Bible is my constant companion. It lights the way for my present life, and it opens the gates of heaven to reveal my future. It guides my heart and my mind to the right way of thinking. I pray I will be a faithful student of Your Word.

....

....

....

....

Morning

FACING THE TRUTH

The spirit of a man is the lamp of the LORD,
searching all the inner depths of his heart.

PROVERBS 20:27 NKJV

Lord, thank You for accepting me as I am, where I am today. You see the potential of who I can be, even when I can't see it. Show me the things in my heart that You want to change. Open my eyes; I don't want to pretend anymore. Help me see the truth so You can make me new!

....

....

....

....

....

Evening

I BLEW IT

If we confess our sins, He is faithful and just to forgive
us our sins and to cleanse us from all unrighteousness.

1 JOHN 1:9 NKJV

Lord, I blew it today. I wish I could take back my attitude and words. Sometimes it's difficult for me to understand why You still love me. Please forgive me. Your Word promises me cleansing if I confess. Help me remember this the next time I feel frustrated and impatient. Help me exercise my will and choose to respond appropriately to the people You've given me. In Christ's name, amen.

....

....

....

....

Morning

INHERITANCE OF BLESSING

Not rendering evil for evil, or railing for railing: but contrariwise blessing;
knowing that ye are thereunto called, that ye should inherit a blessing.

1 PETER 3:9 KJV

It's my first reaction to strike back when I'm hurt, to complain against people who complain about me. You know those tendencies within me, Father. Turn them inside out, I pray, and may my first reaction instead be always to pray and bless. When I feel that this is too much to ask of me, remind me that You will give back to me countless blessings in return.

....

....

....

....

Evening

FINDING ASSURANCE

I have been crucified with Christ and I no longer live, but
Christ lives in me. The life I now live in the body, I live by faith
in the Son of God, who loved me and gave himself for me.

GALATIANS 2:20 NIV

When people see me, let them see You. Help me avoid confusing who You say I am with self-confidence, arrogance, or pride. My confidence is only because You live in and through me. Give me wisdom to know when to speak and when to listen so others may know You through my actions.

....

....

....

....

....

Morning

PUTTING UP WITH IT!

Being reviled, we bless; being persecuted, we suffer it.

1 CORINTHIANS 4:12 KJV

God, give me patience to put up with all the grief that comes my way! You know the things that push my buttons, that get under my skin. Give me the peace to endure them. I know You will use the situation according to Your will, but it's not so fun to suffer through it! Give me the comfort and encouragement I need to endure.

....

....

....

....

....

Evening

LIFE FROM A POSITIVE PERSPECTIVE

But you are a chosen people, a royal priesthood, a holy nation,
God's special possession, that you may declare the praises of him
who called you out of darkness into his wonderful light.

1 PETER 2:9 NIV

As I learn who I am in Christ, I realize that I need to look at life from a positive perspective. My life in You is not about what I'm missing or don't have. It's about Your light and life working in and through me. In even the most difficult situations I will find Your goodness in me.

....

....

....

....

....

Morning

HOW DO I LOVE THEE?

For God so loved the world that He gave His only begotten Son, that whoever believes in Him should not perish but have everlasting life.

JOHN 3:16 NKJV

Dear God, *love* is such a little word, just four letters. Most of the time I don't think about the power of that word: how it can move mountains, calm storms, heal lepers, redeem a sinner. That word saved me from hell. I love You, Lord. Let me never stop counting the ways. Amen.

....

....

....

....

....

Evening

THE BEST ROUTE

I will instruct you and teach you in the way you should go; I will guide you with My eye.

PSALM 32:8 NKJV

Lord, thank You for placing me on a new path and daily offering guidance for each confusing moment and every trouble. I'm so glad You don't expect me to figure out some difficult road map. When it comes to doing Your will, Your Word offers clear direction to all who seek it. You never fail those who seek to follow You faithfully. Let every path I take be one that pleases You.

....

....

....

....

....

Morning
KEEP ME

Keep me as the apple of the eye, hide me under the shadow of thy wings.
PSALM 17:8 KJV

Dear Father, in the scurry of life, I often forget to be thankful for important things. So many times You've shielded my family from physical harm, and I didn't know it until later. Although we are the apple of Your eye, I realize we're not immune to trauma and disaster. I'm grateful that You care about us and that the only way something can touch us is after it's passed Your gentle inspection. Amen.

....

....

....

....

....

Evening
TO LIVE IN CHRIST

Anyone who belongs to Christ has become a new person. The old life is gone; a new life has begun!
2 CORINTHIANS 5:17 NLT

In Your love and mercy You gave me life. I was lost and alone, but You found me. You picked me up and gave me all the benefits of Your own Son, Jesus. Thank You for Your incredible kindness. All I had to do was believe and receive this gift. Father, continue to make me new each day in Christ.

....

....

....

....

....

Morning
FEEDING MY ENEMIES

Therefore if thine enemy hunger, feed him; if he thirst, give him drink.
ROMANS 12:20 KJV

It's not enough to *forgive* my enemies, Lord; now You ask me to actively do them good—to do whatever I can to meet their needs. I'm hurting so much right now that I can't do this on my own, Father. Show me how You want me to do that, and then give me the strength to do it. May I look for opportunities to help those who have hurt me.

....

....

....

....

....

Evening
LET LOVE RULE

"Live out your God-created identity. Live generously and graciously toward others, the way God lives toward you."
MATTHEW 5:48 MSG

Lord, help me get rid of anger, cruelty, and slander. I have the mind of Christ and can exercise self-control. Show me how to live my life with mercy, kindness, humility, gentleness, and patience. I want to be quick to forgive. Above all, help me let Christ govern my heart. Please forgive me when I forget and take control.

....

....

....

....

....

Morning
WAITING FOR GOD

Say not thou, I will recompense evil;
but wait on the LORD, and he shall save thee.
PROVERBS 20:22 KJV

When a situation arises where wrong has been done, I'm quick to feel that the situation is urgent: I have to do something about it *right now*. Teach me, Lord, to wait for You instead. Give me Your wisdom in these situations, and when the time is right, show me what to say and what to do that will bring glory to You.

....

....

....

....

Evening
COMPASSION

Be kind and compassionate to one another, forgiving
each other, just as in Christ God forgave you.
EPHESIANS 4:32 NIV

Lord, Your compassion for people is great. Create in me a heart of compassion—enlarge my vision so I see and help the poor, the sick, the people who don't know You, and the people whose concerns You lay upon my heart. Help me never be so busy or self-absorbed that I overlook my family and friends who may need my assistance.

....

....

....

....

....

Morning
SIBLING REVELRY

Whoever claims to love God yet hates a brother or sister is a liar.
For whoever does not love their brother and sister, whom they
have seen, cannot love God, whom they have not seen.

1 JOHN 4:20 NIV

Heavenly Father, thank You for my siblings. When the chips are down, I can depend on them. When we were kids, we squabbled a lot; but now, I love getting a call from one of them. They understand me like no one else. I pray we'll always be there for one another. Bless my brothers and sisters today. In Jesus' name, amen.

....

....

....

....

Evening
LOYALTY

"Is this your loyalty to your friend? Why did you not go with your friend?"
2 SAMUEL 16:17 NASB

Lord, I want to be a better friend. Help me be trustworthy, devoted, and reliable. Help me put the desires of my friends before my own. Give me the power of encouragement so that I may be at their sides with a ready word and a shoulder to lean on, with love in my heart and a prayer on my lips. I want to clothe others with the warmth of friendship. Make me a true friend.

....

....

....

....

....

Morning
HE IS WILLING

Jesus reached out his hand and touched the man. "I am willing,"
he said. "Be clean!" Immediately he was cleansed of his leprosy.

MATTHEW 8:3 NIV

Dear God, I am astounded by Your love! For a holy God, sin is *worse* than leprosy. You can't even look upon it. Yet Jesus did. I'm not a leper, but sometimes my face *is* mottled by anger, and I'm missing large chunks of the love, joy, peace, patience, kindness, goodness, faithfulness, gentleness, and self-control that are my birthright in Christ. Again and again, You are willing to reach out and cleanse me with Your amazing love. Thank You, Jesus.

....

....

....

....

Evening
PERFECT COUNSELOR

"He will not speak on His own authority, but whatever He
hears He will speak; and He will tell you things to come."

JOHN 16:13 NKJV

When I seek the advice of many and simply end up more confused, it may be because I haven't first turned to the perfect counselor—You. Even the best human won't always know how to counsel perfectly. No one can direct my paths the way You can, Lord. Thank You, Jesus, for giving me Your Spirit's direction. Help me seek You first and walk in Your counsel.

....

....

....

....

....

Morning
THE OTHER CHEEK

Whosoever shall smite thee on thy right cheek, turn to him the other also.
MATTHEW 5:39 KJV

If someone hurts me, do I really have to ask him to hurt me again somewhere else? That seems like You're asking too much! It goes against everything society teaches me about standing up for myself, about being assertive, about not being a doormat. Teach me what Jesus meant when He said this. Give me a heart that wants to follow His example. . .even when I don't want to.

....

....

....

....

....

....

Evening
CULTIVATING A GOOD ATTITUDE

May the words of my mouth and the meditation of my heart
be pleasing to you, O LORD, my rock and my redeemer.
PSALM 19:14 NLT

Lord, the Bible tells me life and death are in the power of the tongue. Sometimes I say words I don't mean or later regret. Fill my spirit with Your goodness. Your words are healthy to me. Help me control what I say by thinking about what pleases You before I open my mouth.

....

....

....

....

....

Morning
FOLLOWING GOOD

*See that none render evil for evil unto any man; but ever follow
that which is good, both among yourselves, and to all men.*

1 THESSALONIANS 5:15 KJV

Even when I see evil all around me, Lord, help me always follow that which is good rather than evil. Forgive me when I am lured by the fake shininess and beauty that evil displays. Keep me from falling for the tricks of the devil, and keep my feet securely on Your path, the good and right path.

....

....

....

....

....

Evening
GIVING SOMETHING
COMPLETELY TO GOD

*People with their minds set on you, you keep completely whole,
steady on their feet, because they keep at it and don't quit.*

ISAIAH 26:3 MSG

When I pray, I give my concerns to You, but later I find that I've made them my responsibility again. Somewhere in my thinking I stop trusting You and try to work problems out on my own. I don't need to know how You are going to resolve them. Forgive me for making problems bigger, and show me how to give them completely to You.

....

....

....

....

Morning
THE PROMISE KEEPER

For no matter how many promises God has made, they are "Yes" in Christ.
2 CORINTHIANS 1:20 NIV

Dear Father, how many times have I promised to call someone and didn't? How many times have I promised to play dolls with my little girl or read a story to my son and didn't? How many times have I promised to get a certain job done and didn't? Forgive me for breaking those promises. You are a God who keeps His promises, who is faithful from generation to generation. Teach me what it means to be truly faithful. Amen.

....

....

....

....

Evening
A TEACHABLE ATTITUDE

My son, pay attention to what I say; turn your ear to my words.
Do not let them out of your sight, keep them within your heart; for
they are life to those who find them and health to one's whole body.
PROVERBS 4:20–22 NIV

Holy Spirit, I invite You to be my teacher, to lead and guide me in all truth. Show me how to let go of selfish desires and listen to Your direction. I'll go where You want me to go today. Help me focus my energy on Your instruction.

....

....

....

....

....

Morning

MAN'S PLANS, GOD'S PURPOSE

People can make all kinds of plans, but only the LORD's plan will happen.
PROVERBS 19:21 NCV

You know the plans of my mind and the desires of my heart, but as Your Word says, it is Your purpose that will rule the day. Help me step aside if I am blocking Your way. Help me keep confident in Your Word and in Your plan for my life. I await Your instructions for the day.

....

....

....

....

....

Evening

LOVE

[Love] beareth all things, believeth all things,
hopeth all things, endureth all things.
1 CORINTHIANS 13:7 KJV

Give me a loving heart, God. Help me endure hurts, always hoping and believing in the best in others. Remind me that love is an everyday action, not just when I feel like it. Help me show love in words as well. Give me Your eyes to see the true worth of the people around me, and help me always display Your love to them. Thank You for being the perfect example of love.

....

....

....

....

....

....

Morning

THE ETERNAL SECURITY SYSTEM

For He will give His angels [especial] charge over you to accompany and defend and preserve you in all your ways [of obedience and service].

PSALM 91:11 AMPC

Dear Lord, Your Word says that we are protected by Your mighty angels. They accompany us and defend us and preserve us when we are walking in Your way. They keep evil *away*. I know there have been times in my life when You protected me, and I was very aware of it. Thank You, Lord, for the invisible guardians that surround me and defend me. Amen.

....

....

....

....

Evening

UNDESERVED PAIN

But if you bear patiently with suffering [which results] when you do right and that is undeserved, it is acceptable and pleasing to God.

1 PETER 2:20 AMPC

Lord, the joys of Your kingdom and pain don't seem compatible, yet in Your own sacrifice they clearly draw together. Your love does not deny the reality of hurt. I can't understand it all, but You promise that patiently putting up with undeserved pain still has a purpose. I please You when I untiringly bear each trial, however large or small. Help me give You that joy today, Jesus.

....

....

....

....

....

Morning
SPIRITUAL GUARDRAILS

Stay alert! Watch out for your great enemy, the devil. He prowls around like a roaring lion, looking for someone to devour.
1 PETER 5:8 NLT

Dear God, help me erect proper boundaries in my life. I don't want to fall prey to a sin simply because I wasn't being careful. Just like guardrails on a dangerous mountain highway, boundaries in my life keep me closer to the center and farther away from the cliffs. Let me cooperate with Your grace by maintaining a careful lifestyle and a discerning spirit. In Christ's name, amen.

Evening
A WOMAN WHO FEARS THE LORD

Favour is deceitful, and beauty is vain: but a woman that feareth the LORD, she shall be praised.
PROVERBS 31:30 KJV

God, I want to be a Proverbs 31 woman. My focus should not be on external beauty or the clothing and jewelry that I wear. Rather, may others notice my heart that is forever seeking You. I want nothing more than to be known as a woman of God. Protect me from vanity. Outward beauty is not lasting, but a beautiful spirit is. I meditate upon Your Word now, Lord. I want to honor You. Amen.

Morning
QUARRELS

Forbearing one another, and forgiving one another, if any man have
a quarrel against any: even as Christ forgave you, so also do ye.
COLOSSIANS 3:13 KJV

Quarrels come so easily some days, Lord, especially with the people I live and work with the most closely. Remind me that Christ has forgiven me for far greater offenses, and help me bite my tongue before I start an argument. When I do stumble, help me humbly ask for forgiveness from the other person. Grant me freedom in my relationships so I am not distracted by bitterness.

....

....

....

....

Evening
KEEPING PROMISES TO MYSELF

Each of you must take responsibility for doing
the creative best you can with your own life.
GALATIANS 6:5 MSG

Lord, You created me for a specific purpose. I make promises to myself and think it's okay not to keep them. Help me remember that I'm responsible to You for how my life turns out. Help me keep the commitments I've set, and give me the courage to accomplish them. Remind me that it's okay to do good things for myself that help me become the person You created me to be.

....

....

....

....

....

Morning

RULE OF LOVE

*"To him who sits on the throne and to the Lamb be praise
and honor and glory and power, for ever and ever!"*
REVELATION 5:13 NIV

Dear Lord, You are Lord of the universe, yet You left Your throne and
came down to earth to be near us. You are the giver and sustainer of life,
yet You sacrificed Your Son to save us. There is no precedent for this kind
of love. What You did for us makes no earthly sense. But You did it, and I
am forever grateful. Amen.

....

....

....

....

....

Evening

A FUTURE FOR ME

*Consider the blameless, observe the upright;
a future awaits those who seek peace.*
PSALM 37:37 NIV

Lord, I am Your child, a child of peace. When someone strikes me on the left
cheek, I turn my head and give them the other. I can only do this through
Your power. Nothing can harm me when I am living so close to You. Now,
with the next breath I take, give me the gift of stillness, of silence, as I put
my future, my hopes, my dreams into Your capable hands.

....

....

....

....

Morning
TENDERHEARTED

And be ye kind one to another, tenderhearted, forgiving one another, even as God for Christ's sake hath forgiven you.
Ephesians 4:32 KJV

The world may look at a tender heart as a weakness, but You know better, God. Your heart is tender toward me, and You are quick to extend grace and mercy. Give me a tender heart, I pray. Guard my heart so that it won't become calloused to the hurts and evils of the world. Fill me with Your kindness, gentleness, compassion, and sincerity so that I can forgive others just as I have been forgiven.

....

....

....

....

Evening
WHEN I'M TEMPTED TO TAKE SHORTCUTS

For we cannot oppose the truth, but must always stand for the truth.
2 Corinthians 13:8 NLT

God, I know it isn't right to take moral shortcuts. You have given me values of honor, integrity, and truth. Help me never compromise. Although others may act without integrity, it's not worth the price of my relationship with You to follow their example. You bless me because I choose what is right and just. Thank You for reminding me of the way I need to go.

....

....

....

....

....

Morning
MOTHER'S DAY

"As one whom his mother comforts, so I will comfort you."
ISAIAH 66:13 NASB

Dear Lord, I thank You today for my mother. No one has loved me like she has. From before I was born, through sickness and rebellion, and even when I was miles away, she has loved me. You blessed me greatly when You gave me to this woman. I praise You for her gentleness, generosity, and quiet strength. I pray that You would bless her today, Lord, with the awareness of how her love and Yours have made a difference in eternity. Amen.

....

....

....

....

Evening
KEEPING COMMITMENTS TO FRIENDS

You yourself must be an example to them by doing good works of every kind.
Let everything you do reflect the integrity and seriousness of your teaching.
TITUS 2:7 NLT

I don't mean to take advantage of others, but I've done it. Jesus, open my eyes to see that I hurt my friends when I'm late, cancel, or just don't show up. Let me see this before it's too late to keep my commitments. Teach me how to schedule for interruptions and still keep the appointments that are most important on the schedule.

....

....

....

....

....

Morning
OVERCOMING

Be not overcome of evil, but overcome evil with good.
ROMANS 12:21 KJV

When darkness seems to be attacking me from all sides, Lord, give me Your strength so that I can rise above the world's evil. Make Your Spirit strong in me so that I can feel Your presence near. Give me the words to say and the things to do to bring Your goodness to every situation. Use me in whatever way You can for Your will to be done. I know I'm on the winning side!

....

....

....

....

....

Evening
WHOLENESS AND RIGHT LIVING

Do not be wise in your own eyes; fear the LORD and shun evil.
This will bring health to your body and nourishment to your bones.
PROVERBS 3:7–8 NIV

Lord, help me be a person who takes care of herself. As I look to Your wisdom for right living, may I enjoy a healthy body. Help me to make wise decisions and to be a good steward of myself, the "temple" You have given me. Help me to never abuse my body but to care for it as You would want me to.

....

....

....

....

....

....

Morning

IN ANY AND EVERY SITUATION

From the fruit of their mouth a person's stomach is filled;
with the harvest of their lips they are satisfied.

PROVERBS 18:20 NIV

Dear Lord, right now my body is well rested, and I confess that I confuse that physical contentment with spiritual health. And at other times I have believed the lie that aches, pains, and sickness mean You have withdrawn Your hand of blessing from me. I am complete in Christ, regardless of my circumstances. Help me live in the light of eternity, unswayed by bank balances, buffets, or blood tests. Amen.

....

....

....

....

Evening

HOPE IN CHRIST

For as in Adam all die, even so in Christ all shall be made alive.

1 CORINTHIANS 15:22 NKJV

Lord, no matter how impossible it is for us to escape death, it still does not have the last word. You sent Jesus to overthrow death and offer life to those who put their faith in Him. The "unchangeable" pattern of death died in a moment of sacrifice, when Your Son gave His life for our sin. I have no greater hope than this, Lord. Help me cling to You alone, no matter what I face.

....

....

....

....

....

Morning
PASSION AND PURPOSE

In Him also we have obtained an inheritance, being predestined according to the purpose of Him who works all things according to the counsel of His will.
EPHESIANS 1:11 NKJV

Father, monotony is wearing away at my sense of purpose. I know there are parts of our lives that are not particularly fulfilling. Yet living without passion or purpose isn't what You had in mind for us. Show me how to find meaning in my everyday life. Open my eyes to the subtle nuances of joy folded into every hour. I put my longings into Your hands. Amen.

....

....

....

....

....

Evening
CONSISTENT LOVE

A friend loves at all times.
PROVERBS 17:17 NKJV

All I need is love! But when I look at my past, I wonder if *I've* always loved my friends. I mean that constant, undying, unyielding love: the kind that You show for us. Forgive me, Lord, for times that I was so caught up in the busyness of my day that I did not show love to a friend who really needed it. Lord, fill me and my friends with Your love, and help us to let it flow freely to all we meet.

....

....

....

....

Morning

GOD'S CHILDREN

Be ye therefore followers of God, as dear children.

EPHESIANS 5:1 KJV

Brothers and sisters often bicker and squabble. My siblings and I are no exception. But remind me, dear God, that Your children should be following You, not fighting with each other. Grant us an abundance of grace when we are dealing with each other, and help us keep our eyes solely on You as we work through difficulties. If we are following Your will, we will be blessed beyond imagination.

....

....

....

....

Evening

GOD'S COMMITMENT TO ME

Remember his covenant forever—the commitment
he made to a thousand generations.

1 CHRONICLES 16:15 NLT

Lord, I want the whole world to know what You have done for me. You have changed my life and set me free. I was lost and alone, and You found me. Everything I need is in You. You created me and crowned me with Your glory. You take responsibility for me, whether I succeed or fail. From the beginning of time, every promise You have made, You have kept. Generation after generation depends on You, just as I do.

....

....

....

....

....

Morning
MERCIFUL

Be ye therefore merciful, as your Father also is merciful.
LUKE 6:36 KJV

Father, I am so thankful for Your mercy, and I am thankful for Your gift of grace—but You know that it is sometimes difficult for me to show mercy to others. It's especially hard for me to be merciful when I see someone making the same mistake over and over again or committing the same sin again and again. But right now I pray that You make me like You. Help me show Your mercy to everyone—with no exceptions.

....
....
....
....

Evening
HEART GUARD

Be anxious for nothing, but in everything by prayer and supplication, with thanksgiving, let your requests be made known to God; and the peace of God, which surpasses all understanding, will guard your hearts and minds through Christ Jesus.
PHILIPPIANS 4:6–7 NKJV

When my heart's hurting, I should pray, Lord. How often do I remember that—or feel like praying when my mind's distracted with worry? Trust in You offers an influx of peace and hope, no matter what I'm facing. Send Your Spirit to my heart. I need Your peace to guard me day by day.

....
....
....
....
....

Morning
CHEERFULNESS

"Be of good cheer, daughter."
MATTHEW 9:22 NKJV

Jesus, I can't imagine You as a solemn man. I believe You enjoyed life immensely, and I know You brought joy to those around You. Why else would "sinners and tax collectors" want to eat with You (as Your enemies pointed out)? Your mission on this planet was sacred and grave, but I believe Your demeanor in everyday life was buoyant and pleasant. Help me pattern my daily attitude after Your example and take heed of Your command to "be of good cheer." Let me reflect You by the way I live. Amen.

....

....

....

....

Evening
THE FIRST PRIORITY

"'Love the Lord your God with all your heart and with all your soul and with all your mind.' This is the first and greatest commandment."
MATTHEW 22:37–38 NIV

Father, You are my everything! Without You, I wouldn't be here. Forgive me for allowing so many other things to squeeze between me and You. Help me become more diligent in my time with You. It fills me with the strength I need to make it day after day. I never want to take our relationship for granted.

....

....

....

....

Morning

LIVING IN THE NOW

*Therefore do not worry about tomorrow, for tomorrow will
worry about itself. Each day has enough trouble of its own.*

MATTHEW 6:34 NIV

I can't change the past, but I think about it a lot. It's a waste of time, and
I hate for my mind to go there. Lord, help me focus on today. Help me
keep my attention on the priorities You have given me. Help me live in
the present. Show me what I can do today to make an eternal difference.

....

....

....

....

....

Evening

SEMPER PARATUS

*"But rise and stand on your feet; for I have appeared to you
for this purpose, to make you a minister and a witness."*

ACTS 26:16 NKJV

God, today I have felt like a concrete footing when the forms get removed.
I confess that I've been depending on the faith and scripture knowledge
of people around me instead of developing my own. When I stand before
You, You will see only *me*. I long to hear You say, *"Well done."* Increase my
faith and devotion to You. Amen.

....

....

....

....

....

Morning

SHIELDED

*Above all, taking the shield of faith, wherewith ye shall
be able to quench all the fiery darts of the wicked.*
EPHESIANS 6:16 KJV

Lord, You tell me that my faith is a shield that will protect me from evil.
Right now I ask You to reinforce that shield. Give me a greater, stronger
faith so that I will be ready when I go through difficult times, when Satan
is shooting his fiery darts directly at me. I will not live in fear about this
possibility, but I will stand on Your promises.

....

....

....

....

....

Evening

WHEN OTHERS FAIL ME

*Make allowance for each other's faults, and forgive anyone who offends
you. Remember, the LORD forgave you, so you must forgive others.*
COLOSSIANS 3:13 NLT

When others fail me, it makes me feel unimportant. Remind me of the times
when circumstances were out of my control and I missed a commitment
and failed someone. Fill me with compassion and understanding for their
situation. Help me get over it and show them Your love.

....

....

....

....

....

Morning
ESSENTIAL JESUS

They replied, "Believe in the Lord Jesus, and you
will be saved—you and your household."
ACTS 16:31 NIV

Lord, I see in myself the tendency to become a Pharisee: to add rules to the essential simplicity of the Gospel. But You remind me of Acts 16:31. Believe in the Lord Jesus. Be saved. That's it. It's not esoteric knowledge; it's not an unattainable level of enlightenment; it's not dressing a certain way; it's not a thousand-mile pilgrimage: it's just You, Jesus. Help me stay true to this message by staying close to You. Amen.

....

....

....

....

Evening
THE WAY OF PEACE

The fruit of that righteousness will be peace;
its effect will be quietness and confidence forever.
ISAIAH 32:17 NIV

You promise I can live in quietness and confidence, Lord. As I believe in You, even when I cannot see the results of faith, I grow the tree of righteousness. Soon it will flower into quietness and confidence, and my life will be blessed. Thank You, Jesus, for Your faithfulness to me. When I can't see the path ahead, You point me in the right direction, and I am blessed in Your way of peace forever.

....

....

....

....

Morning
GOD'S GENTLENESS

Thou hast also given me the shield of thy salvation:
and thy gentleness hath made me great.

2 SAMUEL 22:36 KJV

Father God, when I think about Your gift of salvation to me, I think about the mighty work that Your grace through the death of Jesus Christ does in my life. But there's another side to it. God, thank You for Your gentleness that makes me strong enough to rise above every trial that comes my way. It's because I am saved that I can be free to stand and not be afraid.

....

....

....

....

....

Evening
SACRIFICES

You were taught to be made new in your hearts, to become a new person.
That new person is made to be like God—made to be truly good and holy.

EPHESIANS 4:23–24 NCV

Lord, help me spend my time wisely on the things that matter most. Day-to-day things are continually in my face, screaming for my attention, but there are also things that are eternal, like people. Help me realize my time spent for eternal things, like spending time with others, is not a sacrifice but a reward.

....

....

....

....

Morning
QUIET AND GENTLE

*The unfading beauty of a gentle and quiet
spirit. . . is of great worth in God's sight.*
1 PETER 3:4 NIV

God, I read in Your Word that You value spirits that are gentle and quiet.
At times, this is so hard for me, Lord! I'm not a pushover, but I do have my
own opinions about things. Sometimes it is so hard to keep quiet or speak
softly. Yet, Lord, You know that I want to be that way. Teach me, Lord, how
to be quiet and gentle. Amen.

....

....

....

....

....

Evening
THE RIGHT TIME

People can make all kinds of plans, but only the LORD's plan will happen.
PROVERBS 19:21 NCV

Father, there's so much I want to do, but I just don't know when to do it.
Your timing is everything. You have ordered my steps, and You know the
way that I should go. I ask the Holy Spirit to lead and guide me. Give me
assurance and peace to know when it's time to step forward. Thank You for
making everything happen in Your time, not mine.

....

....

....

....

....

Morning
GOD'S ARMOR

But let us, who are of the day, be sober, putting on the breastplate
of faith and love; and for an helmet, the hope of salvation.
1 THESSALONIANS 5:8 KJV

Father, remind me not to venture out into life's temptations and trials without first putting on Your armor, especially the breastplate of faith and love and the helmet of Your salvation. Teach me to grab hold of these gifts and harness the power that You offer through them. Give me the opportunity to use these pieces of armor to bless others, protecting them against the power of evil.

....

....

....

....

Evening
GOD'S WORKS

He has made His wonderful works to be remembered;
the LORD is gracious and full of compassion.
PSALM 111:4 NKJV

When sorrow fills my heart, the world becomes tiny if I focus on my own pain. But You have given me so many wonderful things in the world to remind me of Your grace and compassion. Remind me that You love all Your children, including me. I know You have many more works to do in my life. Keep my eyes open for them as I cling to You now and forever.

....

....

....

....

....

Morning
THE ALREADY-DONE LIST

The LORD appeared to him long ago, saying, "I have loved you with an everlasting love; therefore I have drawn you out with kindness."
JEREMIAH 31:3 NASB

Dear God, plans and schedules help me stay focused and productive. But I know I have missed opportunities because I was too busy checking off my to-do list. And I know that I often base my self-worth on how much I have accomplished. Help me remember that I can never *do* enough to earn Your love. I am already loved, completely and eternally. The only thing that really needed doing, You did on the cross. Thank You, Lord.

....

....

....

....

Evening
UNMET EXPECTATIONS

Let us hold tightly without wavering to the hope we affirm, for God can be trusted to keep his promise.
HEBREWS 10:23 NLT

Lord, my expectations were high, and I'm so disappointed in what looks to be the outcome of this situation. Help me remember that You are in control. I've given this situation to You. Help me let go of it once again. You are faithful and just, and You always deliver what You promise. It doesn't look like what I expected, but I'm learning that Your way is always better in the end.

....

....

....

....

Morning
A QUIET QUEST

"In quietness and confidence shall be your strength."
ISAIAH 30:15 NKJV

Dear Lord, we find great blessings when spending time with people. But I need Your help to embrace solitude too. Let me see the value in spending some time alone, refreshing my spirit in the quiet. Not only do I need to spend quiet time with You in personal worship but I need to incorporate into my daily routine those pockets of time when the music is off and the computer is down. Help me make quiet times my quest. Amen.

....
....
....
....
....

Evening
PURSUING MY DREAM

I press toward the goal for the prize of the upward call of God in Christ Jesus.
PHILIPPIANS 3:14 NKJV

You gave me a gift, and I want to use it to begin the work You have for me to do. Jesus knew His mission while on the earth, and He completed it. Father, give me the drive, power, and determination to accomplish my mission. I am committed and ready to pursue my dream. Thank You for the courage to move forward. I am stepping out in faith today.

....
....
....
....
....

Morning
LIT

Let your loins be girded about, and your lights burning.
LUKE 12:35 KJV

When everywhere I look I see only darkness, please, Lord, turn on the lights in my heart. Show me ways to share that illumination with everyone around me. When Your light burns, darkness flees. Use me. Light me, I pray.

....

....

....

....

....

....

Evening
JESUS' EXAMPLE

If we confess our sins, he is faithful and just and will forgive us our sins and purify us from all unrighteousness.
1 JOHN 1:9 NIV

When I look at forgiveness, I look at You, Jesus. Help me reflect Your love, Lord, by forgiving those who wrong me. In my own power, I weakly want revenge. But through Your Spirit, poured out in my life, I follow Your loving example. Forgive me for all my sins, Lord, and make me faithful and pure in You.

....

....

....

....

....

Morning

WIDE AWAKE

Therefore let us not sleep, as do others; but let us watch and be sober.
1 THESSALONIANS 5:6 KJV

You know how tired I am, God. You know how weary I am of facing troubles and challenges. Help me resist surrendering to my exhaustion. Send godly friends into my life that can encourage me to continue on the path that You have laid for Your children. Keep me wide awake and alert, focused always on You.

....

....

....

....

....

Evening

TO SEE IT THROUGH

The way of the good person is like the light of dawn, growing brighter and brighter until full daylight.
PROVERBS 4:18 NCV

Lord, my life isn't turning out as I thought it would. I've found rough waters at every turn. You never said it would be easy, but You have promised to do more than I can imagine. Help me see this dream through to reality. Show me what it looks like from Your perspective. Help me avoid falling short and rise to the level You desire me to reach.

....

....

....

....

....

Morning
CRY IN THE NIGHT

"Then you call on the name of your god, and I will call on the name of the LORD. The god who answers by fire—he is God."

1 KINGS 18:24 NIV

Dear Lord, there is never a time I cry out to You and You are not instantly listening. You are never too busy to hear me. Help me examine my heart when I fear that You are silent, and forgive my sins. I long to stand before You, complete and unashamed. I know I am never alone. Amen.

....

....

....

....

....

Evening
REMOVING THE LIMITS

Listen to my voice in the morning, LORD. Each morning I bring my requests to you and wait expectantly.

PSALM 5:3 NLT

Father, You have promised to hear me when I pray and honor me as I serve You. We're doing this together. I am removing the limits that have constrained me in the past. It doesn't matter what other people think; my heart is tuned to Your voice. I hear Your words, and I determine never to follow a discouraging voice. Nothing is impossible with You.

....

....

....

....

....

Morning

DELIVERED

Because he hath set his love upon me, therefore will I deliver him:
I will set him on high, because he hath known my name.

PSALM 91:14 KJV

When troubles threaten to drown me, loving Lord, reach down and save me. Deliver me from the floods. Rescue me from the fire. Remove me from the storm. Protect me from the violence. Pick me up and set me on a high place where I will be safe in Your presence. I know my Deliverer is coming.

....
....
....
....
....

Evening

NEEDING ENCOURAGEMENT

May our Lord Jesus Christ himself and God our Father, who loved
us and by his grace gave us eternal encouragement and good hope,
encourage your hearts and strengthen you in every good deed and word.

2 THESSALONIANS 2:16–17 NIV

Lord, I need encouragement. Will You please inspire my heart and strengthen me in everything I say and do? I need Your truth to lift my spirit and help me soar. Let me be like an eagle that glides on the wind. Give me the courage and energy I need to keep going, even when I'm weary.

....
....
....
....
....

Morning

BLESSED ARE THE FLEXIBLE

This is the day the LORD has made; we will rejoice and be glad in it.

PSALM 118:24 NKJV

Flexibility is a struggle for me, God. I don't like interruptions in my routine. It's challenging for me to accept a rerouting of my day. Still, sometimes You have to reorganize for me, because I haven't recognized Your promptings. Or maybe there's someone You need me to meet or a disaster You want me to avoid. Help me accept the detours in my plan today, aware of Your sovereignty over all. Amen.

....

....

....

....

Evening

PRAISE FOR THE FATHER OF COMPASSION

Blessed be the God and Father of our Lord Jesus Christ,
the Father of mercies and God of all comfort.

2 CORINTHIANS 1:3 NKJV

Lord, You love us so much. Fill me with that love to overflowing. Give me a compassionate heart. Lead me to the concern You would like me to champion for You, whether it be working in a soup kitchen, helping the homeless, or adopting a missionary couple. Lead me in prayer as I go down on my knees and intercede for others in distress.

....

....

....

....

....

Morning

PRESERVED

The LORD preserveth all them that love him.

PSALM 145:20 KJV

Preserve me, God; keep me safe—that's what I'm asking of You. Guard my physical body, my head, and my heart. Grant me traveling mercies as I move from place to place. Take away my anxiety, my worries, and my woes. I love You—and I need Your help now. I can't do it alone.

....

....

....

....

....

Evening

PERSEVERANCE IN PRAYER

As you know, we count as blessed those who have persevered. You have heard of Job's perseverance and have seen what the Lord finally brought about. The Lord is full of compassion and mercy.

JAMES 5:11 NIV

I feel like I've been praying forever for a situation that doesn't seem to be changing, Lord. I'm on my knees in prayer while the entire world dissolves around me. I know You're in control. You know all things. So once again, I lift my concern up to You, confident that You will handle the situation in Your timing.

....

....

....

....

....

Morning
THE LIAR

*If we confess our sins, he is faithful and just to forgive us
our sins, and to cleanse us from all unrighteousness.*
1 JOHN 1:9 KJV

Dear God, someone lied to me today. It was a small lie, but it felt like a brick had been thrown at me. I realized, Lord, that the burden had become mine because I chose to carry it. A small lie became in my heart the equal sins of anger, resentment, and despair. Show me how to lay that ugly thing at the foot of the cross and pick up joy instead. Amen.

....

....

....

....

Evening
BLESSING ENEMIES

Wish good for those who harm you; wish them well and do not curse them.
ROMANS 12:14 NCV

God, I pray that you will bless those who have not been kind to me. You know who they are. Give me the blessing of forgiving others as You always forgive me. Help me resist repaying evil with evil, responding instead with kindness, for that is what You would have me do. Give me the strength to be good to them, even helpful, and to keep my anger and frustration at bay. Bless their lives, Lord.

....

....

....

....

....

Morning

TRUE HOMELAND PERSPECTIVE

They agreed that they were foreigners and nomads here on earth. Obviously people who say such things are looking forward to a country they can call their own.

HEBREWS 11:13–14 NLT

God, I want to live with an eternal perspective. Heaven is an actual place, as real as this earth and far more lasting. When I live like this earth is the ultimate goal, I tend toward selfish indulgence. When I remember that heaven is my real destination, I value the lasting things of true importance. Remind me to keep an eye toward Your heavenly kingdom. Amen.

....

....

....

....

Evening

COMPASSION FOR THE HUNGRY

Make me truly happy by agreeing wholeheartedly with each other, loving one another, and working together with one mind and purpose.

PHILIPPIANS 2:2 NLT

With Your compassion, today I reach out to the hungry here and abroad. Show me where my hands can be used to help those in need. I want to serve others in the name of Jesus Christ, as You have called us to do. Open a door for me. Show me what I can do to make this world a better place.

....

....

....

....

....

Morning
THE ONE NEEDFUL THING

I will be fully satisfied as with the richest of foods;
with singing lips my mouth will praise you.
PSALM 63:5 NIV

Dear Father, You are the giver of good gifts, but I confess that I'm often on the lookout for more. Thank You for the things I have, but help me control my desire for more. No *thing* I have will define me, and neither will it make me complete. Only You can make me complete, Jesus. Amen.

....

....

....

....

....

Evening
COMMUNITY PEACE AND
UNDERSTANDING

The weapons we fight with are not the weapons of the world.
On the contrary, they have divine power to demolish strongholds.
2 CORINTHIANS 10:4 NIV

God, through the divine power of Your Spirit and Your Word, I pray for my neighborhood. Touch each heart with Your peace and understanding. You know what each family needs. Help me be an encouragement to them. Be with me as I take a prayer walk around this neighborhood, lifting each family up to Your heavenly throne.

....

....

....

....

Morning
ALIVE AND BLESSED

The LORD will preserve him, and keep him alive; and he shall be blessed upon the earth: and thou wilt not deliver him unto the will of his enemies.
PSALM 41:2 KJV

Sickness. . .violence. . .exhaustion. . .stress—our world is full of dangers. Some of the dangers I face are truly life threatening, Lord. But I don't want to live a life of fear. You call me to be bold and fearless. Thank You that You've promised to not only save my life but also bless me.

....

....

....

....

....

Evening
COMFORT FOR THE SUFFERING

[Jesus said,] "You are the light of the world— like a city on a hilltop that cannot be hidden."
MATTHEW 5:14 NLT

Dearest Christ, I pray for Your bright light to spread out into the world. For Your love to reach the ends of the earth. Give comfort to those who suffer from abuse and violence. Touch them with Your healing light and guard them with Your protective hand. Give them assurance that You are there. Allow them to feel Your presence, hear Your voice, feel Your touch.

....

....

....

....

....

Morning

THE PERFECTIONIST TRAP

As for God, His way is perfect.
2 SAMUEL 22:31 AMPC

Dear Lord, I am so glad that You are such a high, mighty, and separate God. We can only make gods in our own image. We could never imagine You, Lord. I would never bow to Artemis or Baal or Thor, but I realized just now in my perfectionism I am setting up another god to worship—myself. Always doing, striving, perfecting, tweaking my little universe. Please help me be content with imperfection. Only You are perfect, and I am complete, now, in You. Amen.

....

....

....

....

Evening

BLESSED!

"Blessed are those whose transgressions are forgiven, whose sins are covered."
ROMANS 4:7 NIV

Because my sins are covered by Your blood, Jesus, I am blessed. I am forgiven, and You've helped me forgive others too. No matter what I experience today, Your blessings never alter. You do not change Your mind and decide not to love or forgive me. Thank You for giving me Your blessing, because I need it daily. Help me cling to Your love. No matter what I face, I want to remember that the forgiveness of sin is the most important gift You offer.

....

....

....

....

....

Morning
NEVER FORSAKEN

*For the LORD loveth judgment, and forsaketh
not his saints; they are preserved for ever.*

PSALM 37:28 KJV

Father God, I've experienced abandonment in my life. The experience left me feeling empty, alone, helpless. Thank You, Father, that You will never forsake me; You will never abandon me. I am grateful for the security this promise affords me. You will keep me safe forever in Your loving arms that are big enough and strong enough to hold me and all my issues.

....

....

....

....

....

Evening
FINDING YOUR GIFT

Don't act thoughtlessly, but understand what the Lord wants you to do.

EPHESIANS 5:17 NLT

Lord, I'm looking for direction. I'm not sure how You want me to serve You. So many times I feel so inadequate, like others can do things better than I ever could. But I know those feelings are not of You. Help me understand, Lord, how You want me to serve, what You want me to do. Worrying not about pleasing others but about pleasing You, I will do so all to Your glory.

....

....

....

....

....

Morning
JUST DO IT

But be doers of the word, and not hearers only, deceiving yourselves.
JAMES 1:22 NKJV

Dear Lord, I want an obedient heart. Sometimes, when You speak to me, I want to postpone what You're telling me to do. That means I don't trust You or I want my own way, neither of which is good. A child ought to obey her parents because she acknowledges their right to direct her and because she trusts the love behind the words. Help me, Lord, to embrace that kind of attitude when You speak to me. In Christ's name, amen.

....

....

....

....

Evening
CLOTHED WITH COMPASSION

Therefore, as God's chosen people, holy and dearly loved, clothe yourselves with compassion, kindness, humility, gentleness and patience.
COLOSSIANS 3:12 NIV

As I get down on my knees, I wrap myself within the cloak of compassion. I bring to You specific concerns, knowing that You hear my prayer, confident that You will answer. As I rise from the place of prayer, may Your kindness, humility, gentleness, and patience shine through me and lighten the hearts of others. I want to be Your servant. Help me change the world.

....

....

....

....

....

Morning

SAVED FROM ALL EVIL

The LORD shall preserve thee from all evil: he shall preserve thy soul.
PSALM 121:7 KJV

Evil comes in so many shapes and forms. Sometimes it comes into my life disguised, and by the time I recognize its presence, my soul is already in danger. When this happens, Father, be my rescuer (even when I don't ask for rescuing!). Thank You, Lord, that You are always watching over me—and You will protect me from evil of every kind.

....

....

....

....

....

Evening

BOLD AND DILIGENT

"Be bold and diligent. And GOD be with you as you do your best."
2 CHRONICLES 19:11 MSG

I want to do my best, knowing that You are with me all the way. Help me be brave. Help me avoid panic. Neither fear nor anxiety is of You. I need to focus on You, to build up my faith and my confidence. Help me never deviate from my course. I am ready to listen to Your voice. Lead me, gentle Shepherd, where You want me to go.

....

....

....

....

....

....

Morning

MY HIDING PLACE

Thou art my hiding place; thou shalt preserve me from trouble;
thou shalt compass me about with songs of deliverance.

PSALM 32:7 KJV

Heavenly Father, when the world seems like a dangerous place, when anxieties rush at me everywhere I turn, be my hiding place. Be by my side and let me run into Your arms. Wrap me up in Your embrace and sing to me Your sweet song of deliverance. May I never think I'm so self-sufficient that I reject Your comfort and protection.

....

....

....

....

Evening

IN GOD'S STRENGTH

I have strength for all things in Christ Who empowers me [I am
ready for anything and equal to anything through Him Who infuses
inner strength into me; I am self-sufficient in Christ's sufficiency].

PHILIPPIANS 4:13 AMPC

It's amazing—I can do all things through You! You give me the power, the energy, the ways and means! As I lie here, in Your presence, I feel all the energy emanating from You. Give me that strength I need to accomplish my goals. Plant the words "I can do all things through God—He strengthens me!" in my heart forever.

....

....

....

....

....

Morning
FRESH INK

I lean on, rely on, and trust in Your word.
PSALM 119:42 AMPC

Dear Lord, I pray for insight today as I read Your Word. I want to know You better today than I did yesterday and better tomorrow than I do today. Thank You for the Holy Spirit, who guides me as I read. I pray for a fresh filling of that Spirit. I thank You for the verses I will read today and how they will speak to me, as if You wrote them for me this morning, as if the ink is still wet. Amen.

....

....

....

....

Evening
HONORING OTHERS WITH MY MOUTH

Don't try to impress others. Be humble,
thinking of others as better than yourselves.
PHILIPPIANS 2:3 NLT

I don't need fancy words to impress others. I only need words guided by the mind of Christ. Help me, Lord, to honor others with my speech. I want to lift people up, not bring them down. I want to bring joy to the hearts of others, not sorrow. Give me a better attitude, positive words, and encouraging remarks. Guard my mouth and, when necessary, put Your hand upon it to keep it shut.

....

....

....

....

....

Morning

THE SIMPLE LIFE

*Aspire to lead a quiet life, to mind your own
business, and to work with your own hands.*

1 THESSALONIANS 4:11 NKJV

Dear God, everyone yearns for simplicity. We yearn for a more laid-back lifestyle. Lord, I need to simplify my goals in my relationships and work. Doing so will give me a clearer focus. In my spiritual life, a little simplifying might be good too. Help me concentrate on one or two verses daily, deepening my understanding of You. Lord, help me keep simple goals and a simple faith as I simply live for You. Amen.

....

....

....

....

Evening

PATH OF BLESSING

*All the paths of the LORD are mercy and truth,
to such as keep His covenant and His testimonies.*

PSALM 25:10 NKJV

Keeping Your Word brings mercy and truth in my life, Lord. How can I thank You for calling me to live in Your blessings, Jesus? Though keeping Your Word challenges me, so many blessings come from doing Your will. Even if I fail, Your mercy draws me back to Your way. Your never-failing love does not leave my heart. I don't want to wander from Your side, Lord.

....

....

....

....

....

Morning
A TOWER ON A ROCK

*The God of my rock; in him will I trust: he is my shield,
and the horn of my salvation, my high tower, and my
refuge, my saviour; thou savest me from violence.*

2 SAMUEL 22:3 KJV

You, O Lord, are my place of absolute safety: a high tower built on a rock that will never move. When trials and temptations surround me, teach me to lift my gaze higher. Help me look above all my troubles and see Your tall tower—and then run there as fast as I can!

....

....

....

....

....

Evening
SHELTER IN HIM

*Those who live in the shelter of the Most High
will find rest in the shadow of the Almighty.*

PSALM 91:1 NLT

I want to live in Your place, Lord, and share the blessings of Your rest. Peace, love, and harmony fill my life as I stand by Your side. You offer me every good thing, simply for sticking close to You. May I always find my rest in You, Lord. Show me how to live in Your shelter today.

....

....

....

....

....

Morning

MIRROR, MIRROR

I will praise You, for I am fearfully and wonderfully made.
PSALM 139:14 NKJV

Father, when I look at certain people, all I see is how much I lack in comparison. They seem naturally kinder, more at ease, more fashionable, more attractive. I often spend more time thinking about how other people see me than about how You see me. You made me, sovereign Lord, for Your purposes. Help me trust You and trust that this lump of clay that You are molding is precious in Your sight and in Your hands. Amen.

....

....

....

....

Evening

PERSONAL GRACE

But to each one of us grace has been given as Christ apportioned it.
EPHESIANS 4:7 NIV

You have given me just the right amount of grace, Lord. No matter what I'm doing today, You offer grace for all my wants. No matter what my situation, You help me. Nothing in my life is so awful that You cannot bring blessing from it if I seek Your will. I need only tap into You moment by moment to experience Your touch of grace. Thank You for loving me, Jesus. Help me do Your will today.

....

....

....

....

....

Morning
THE PATH TO JOY

Keep your lives free from the love of money
and be content with what you have.
HEBREWS 13:5 NIV

Lord, wherever I look, I see glossy advertisements. It's difficult to be content when you're bombarded with messages to the contrary. I know that accumulating more stuff isn't the path to joy. You don't bless me so I can indulge myself, but so I can share with others. Let my life be marked by restraint and a deep contentment that's rooted in You, the center of my fulfillment. In Jesus' name, amen.

....

....

....

....

....

Evening
WORLDLY FEARS

"But blessed is the one who trusts in the LORD, whose confidence is in him."
JEREMIAH 17:7 NIV

I am so blessed, for even though I fear many things right now, I trust in You. I refuse to go along with the world, driven by despair, fear, and insecurity. I will not bow to outside pressures. I will live my life with the assurance that You are with me. I will put my confidence in You, for I trust You to look out for me, to always be with me, no matter what.

....

....

....

....

Morning
MY REFUGE

The LORD also will be a refuge for the oppressed, a refuge in times of trouble.
PSALM 9:9 KJV

In times of trouble, Lord, when I feel that the pressure is overwhelming, thank You that You are my Refuge—a place of peace, love, and acceptance. Teach me to seek Your protection at the onset of troubles, rather than trying to handle them on my own. I don't get extra points for trying to stick it out by myself.

....

....

....

....

....

Evening
GIVING FORGIVENESS

"For if you forgive other people when they sin against you, your heavenly Father will also forgive you."
MATTHEW 6:14 NIV

Because You have forgiven me, You also expect me to forgive others, Lord. You don't want me to hold on to the wrongs of others while being forgiven myself. Instead You tell me to take Your love as an example for my life. Make me sensitive to all who hurt me, Lord. Help me love them as You have loved me.

....

....

....

....

....

Morning

WHERE'S YOUR MISSING PIECE?

In Him you have been made complete.

Colossians 2:10 nasb

Dear Lord, the people who still need You don't usually go around with "Unsaved" emblazoned on their T-shirts. Sometimes they look just fine, like they aren't missing anything at all. Lord, this is when I feel most uncertain how to tell them about You. I need Your eyes, Lord, to see exactly where and how deep are their "God-shaped holes." Unbelievers are not complete, despite how they may appear. I trust You to lead me, for You love them so much. Amen.

....

....

....

....

Evening

GOD'S CONTROL

Blessed are those whose help is the God of Jacob, whose hope is in the Lord their God. He is the Maker of heaven and earth, the sea, and everything in them—he remains faithful forever.

Psalm 146:5–6 niv

Lord, You faithfully control all things within this world. Looking to Your creation, I see Your hand in every detail. When pain fills my heart, You are there, healing me with Your love. Thank You, Jesus, for all Your blessings of faithfulness. Keep me mindful of them as I seek to trust in You.

....

....

....

....

....

Morning
TIME MANAGEMENT

Teach us to number our days, that we may gain a heart of wisdom.
PSALM 90:12 NIV

Dear God, it seems I never have enough time. I remember simpler seasons in my life when I could actually complete my to-do lists. There was such satisfaction in having a few stress-free moments. Now, my schedule is filled, and I'm so harried. Holy Spirit, please guide me in this area of my life. I'm asking for Your wisdom. Show me how to manage the hours I have so I can honor You in everything I do. In Christ's name, amen.

....

....

....

....

Evening
GOD'S RESCUE

The LORD makes firm the steps of the one who delights in him; though he may stumble, he will not fall, for the LORD upholds him with his hand.
PSALM 37:23–24 NIV

What a comfort it is, Lord, to know that I may stumble, but I'll never fall flat on my face when I'm in communion with You. Thank You for planting my feet on the right path. I'm only human; I still make serious mistakes. Yet even then, You don't desert me. When I'm walking with You, I need fear nothing.

....

....

....

....

....

Morning
SINGING

But I will sing of thy power; yea, I will sing aloud of thy mercy in the morning: for thou hast been my defence and refuge in the day of my trouble.
PSALM 59:16 KJV

God, You know all my troubles—but today, I'm going to start my day singing. Give me a song of power and mercy that will stay with me all day long, especially when the stresses of the day come. No matter what life throws at me, I want to live with Your joyful melody in my heart until Jesus returns to take me home!

....

....

....

....

Evening
ONE SAVIOR

"He is the one all the prophets testified about, saying that everyone who believes in him will have their sins forgiven through his name."
ACTS 10:43 NLT

No one else can forgive sin as You do, Jesus. Though people help or hurt me, they do not command my soul or my salvation. Remind me of this when life becomes too painful or doubtful. What freedom from sin You brought to me! Nothing on earth gives such cleanness to a soul. Let nothing this side of heaven keep me from faith in You, my Savior.

....

....

....

....

....

Morning
HOPE

Thou art my hiding place and my shield: I hope in thy word.
PSALM 119:114 KJV

God, one of the surest ways to find Your hope is to open up scripture and meditate on Your Word. There I learn that You formed me in my mother's womb, that You love me and cherish me, that You provided a way for me to have an intimate relationship with You through the death, burial, and resurrection of Jesus Christ, and that You have amazing plans for me here and into eternity. Your words fill me with amazing hope, Father.

....

....

....

....

....

Evening
FEARING GOD

"He shows mercy from generation to generation to all who fear him."
LUKE 1:50 NLT

Jesus, because I hold You in awe and respect, your mercy will follow me and all my family members who trust in You. No matter how much we hurt right now, we can trust fully in You. You guide and direct us, no matter how deep the pain, and bring us into the peace only Your love can bring. Pour out Your mercy on us, Jesus. May we trust in You for everything today.

....

....

....

....

....

Morning
MY PRAYER WARRIORS

Always labouring fervently for you in prayers, that ye
may stand perfect and complete in all the will of God.
Colossians 4:12 KJV

I thank You today, Lord, for all the people who have prayed for me. They have lifted me up to the throne of grace, faithfully and passionately. I ask You to bless them today. Strengthen their faith in the invisible power of their work. I ask that You would bring me to their minds today, Lord, for I covet their intercession. Thank You for these faithful warriors. I need them so desperately. Amen.

....

....

....

....

Evening
FAITHFUL LORD

But the Lord is faithful, who will establish
you and guard you from the evil one.
2 Thessalonians 3:3 NKJV

I have felt the attack of the evil one, Lord, many times. His snares have caught me in sin, and even since You took control of my life, his sneak attacks have tried to lure me away. But Satan is a defeated enemy. When I am strong in You, he cannot bypass Your guard. Your strength always defends me successfully. Thank You for protecting me, Jesus. No battle that You fight is ever lost.

....

....

....

....

Morning
SAFE IN THE MIDST OF THE WORLD

I pray not that thou shouldest take them out of the world,
but that thou shouldest keep them from the evil.
JOHN 17:15 KJV

Jesus, You didn't ask that I be physically removed from the earth, so that I'd be immune to the world's temptations and tests. Instead, You asked that God protect me no matter what I face. Thank You, Jesus, that You prayed for *me*.

....

....

....

....

....

Evening
PERFECTION AND PEACE

Mark the perfect man, and behold the upright: for the end of that man is peace.
PSALM 37:37 KJV

Everyone wants to experience peace, Lord. I'll admit I've tried more than one method of obtaining it. You've made it clear that perfection leads to peace. "Impossible," many will say, but You aren't saying we'll never make mistakes. You're simply saying that if we walk according to Your Word and sincerely grow in faith, Your peace will result.

....

....

....

....

....

....

Morning

THE UNVEILING

But we all, with unveiled faces, looking as in a mirror at he glory of the Lord, are being transformed into the same image from glory to glory.
2 CORINTHIANS 3:18 NASB

Lord, I'm wondering what it really means to be complete in Jesus Christ. What does *complete* really mean, for me? Whole. Absolute. Total. Finished. Accomplished. Concluded. Fulfilled. There is nothing left to be done. My transformation from stone to flesh was finished at the cross. The work is done; we are just awaiting the final unveiling. Praise Jesus. Amen.

Evening

ONE REQUIREMENT

For God so loved the world that he gave his one and only Son, that whoever believes in him shall not perish but have eternal life.
JOHN 3:16 NIV

Can it be so simple, Lord? I just have to believe? Your promise of pure faith opens the door to eternal life. I'm glad I don't have to jump through hoops to earn Your love. In Your compassion, You gave Your Son so that all who believe can spend forever with You. Thank You for that eternal outpouring of love. I never want to be separated from You.

Morning
YES AND NO

But let your communication be, Yea, yea; Nay, nay:
for whatsoever is more than these cometh of evil.
MATTHEW 5:37 KJV

God, teach me Your ways so that no evil will take root in my life. Remind me to make my words count, so that my "yes" means yes, and my "no" means no. Make me a person of integrity that others can trust. When people ask me why I do what I do, let me always point them to You.

....

....

....

....

....

Evening
OVERCOMING MOUNTAINS

Truly I tell you, whoever says to this mountain, Be lifted up and
thrown into the sea! and does not doubt at all in his heart but
believes that what he says will take place, it will be done for him.
MARK 11:23 AMPC

The mountains in my life are not made of rock and dirt, Lord. Instead they consist of doubts and fears. They've become as real as any physical barrier. Help my doubting heart, Lord. Keep my eyes on You. Remind me that no mountain is big to You and I've put my faith in the right place.

....

....

....

....

....

Morning
THE WELL OF WORDS

"Whoever drinks the water I give them will never thirst. Indeed, the water I give them will become in them a spring of water welling up to eternal life."
JOHN 4:14 NIV

Lord, sometimes I worry that I'll run out of things to say. Then I remember You created everything out of nothing. You are the author of life, the Word made flesh. Thank You for breathing that same spark of creativity into us. I know that if I keep my eyes fixed on You, I'll never run out of words. There is no end to the ways I can praise You! Amen.

Evening
GOD'S FAITHFULNESS

She tastes and sees that her gain from work [with and for God] is good; her lamp goes not out, but it burns on continually through the night [of trouble, privation, or sorrow, warning away fear, doubt, and distrust].
PROVERBS 31:18 AMPC

The light of Your Spirit is never completely extinguished, Jesus, no matter my predicament. Keep my heart faithful, Lord. Remind me that Your faithfulness and love never fail. Thank You, Jesus, for lighting my way into the future. No matter how many dark things surround me, I need never doubt that Your Spirit leads me in the right direction.

Morning
BACK TO CENTER

Mark out a straight path for your feet so that those who
are weak and lame will not fall but become strong.
HEBREWS 12:13 NLT

Heavenly Father, I need balance in my life. It's one of the hardest things for humans to achieve. We're so prone to lopsidedness, to extremes. Maintaining center is challenging. That's why I need You to straighten me out and help me stay in the narrow way. In those areas of my life where I'm listing to the side, bring me back to center, O Lord. In Jesus' name, amen.

....

....

....

....

Evening
JESUS, MY FRIEND

"You are My friends if you do what I command you."
JOHN 15:14 NASB

How do I show that I'm Your friend, Lord? You tell me right here: obedience shows I really love You. I need to put belief into action. Living faithfully during trials challenges me, Lord, but it also draws me close to You. Our friendship grows in times of trouble as I experience Your trustworthiness and grow in obedience. Help me obey You even when I hurt. You *are* my Best Friend, Lord.

....

....

....

....

....

Morning

TIME MACHINE

*There is a time for everything, and a season
for every activity under the heavens.*

ECCLESIASTES 3:1 NIV

Dear Lord, I have so much work to do and so little time. I always feel like I'm running behind. I know this is not what You want. Jesus was never in a hurry. He had time to do the Father's will. He had time to pray on a mountainside, chat beside a well, sit by a lake and cook a fish with friends. Give me wisdom as I seek to set aside my endless to-do list for Your holy will. Amen.

....

....

....

....

Evening

FOR THE POOR AND NEEDY

*"When you give to the needy, do not let your left hand know what
your right hand is doing, so that your giving may be in secret. Then
your Father, who sees what is done in secret, will reward you."*

MATTHEW 6:3–4 NIV

Lord, I pray today for the poor and needy. Please provide food and water to meet their physical needs, and the Gospel of Jesus Christ and His saving love to fill their souls. Lord, show me where I can give and serve. Use my abilities and finances to help, for Your glory.

....

....

....

....

....

Morning

HOPE TO THE END

Wherefore gird up the loins of your mind, be sober, and hope to the end for the grace that is to be brought unto you at the revelation of Jesus Christ.

1 PETER 1:13 KJV

I have put my hope in Your grace, Lord, which You showed to me through the life of Your Son, Jesus Christ. The account of His death, burial, and resurrection is one that saves me for all eternity. I want to emulate His example of grace-filled living now, in my everyday life. Help me always keep His example as my focus.

....

....

....

....

Evening

PRAISE FOR STRENGTH

To You, O my Strength, I will sing praises; for God is my defense, my God of mercy.

PSALM 59:17 NKJV

When I am weak, Your strength upholds me. When I am afraid, Your courage sustains me. When I am downcast, Your presence lifts me. You are always there for me. How great, how wonderful, how amazing You are, my God, my Friend, my Father. I am here before You, singing endless praises to Your name!

....

....

....

....

....

Morning

HOSPITALITY

Use hospitality one to another without grudging.

1 PETER 4:9 KJV

Dear Lord, I need to improve my skills in hospitality. Because You have blessed me, I need to share with others. In fact, hospitality is one of those virtues the apostle Paul commanded of the church. Sharing my home with others is my Christian duty and also a great way to reach out to unbelievers whom I have befriended. Please don't let me dread hosting others, but rather, help me find ways to make it doable and enjoyable for all. In Jesus' name, amen.

....

....

....

....

Evening

PRAISE TO THE HEAVENLY CREATOR

Bless the LORD, O my soul! O LORD my God, You are very great:
You are clothed with honor and majesty, who cover Yourself with light
as with a garment, who stretch out the heavens like a curtain.

PSALM 104:1–2 NKJV

You made all the planets, the stars, the waters, the land on which I stand. Is nothing too difficult for You? You are wrapped in light, and I come now into that light, to be with You, to revel in Your presence, to praise Your holy name. Surround me with Your arms among these clouds.

....

....

....

....

....

Morning
FIRM

But the Lord is faithful, who shall stablish you, and keep you from evil.
2 Thessalonians 3:3 kjv

God, I know You are faithful. Be my Rock and my firm foothold, and please be the foundation of my life. Make me firm and solid so that I can always resist evil. When my own faith is firmly rooted, then please allow me to help others find their strength in Your faithfulness. Your strength will sustain all Your children!

....

....

....

....

....

Evening
PRAISE SILENCES ENEMIES

Through the praise of children and infants you have established a stronghold against your enemies, to silence the foe and the avenger.
Psalm 8:2 niv

With You on my side, You who holds the heavens in Your hands, You who sustains the entire universe, I need not be afraid of my enemies, of those who wish to harm me, or of the evil one that dogs my steps. With praises to You on my lips and in my heart, my foes are vanquished. You are my great Refuge, my Rock of strength.

....

....

....

....

....

Morning
THE BEACON

No one has seen God at any time. If we love one another,
God abides in us, and His love has been perfected in us.

1 JOHN 4:12 NKJV

Lord, You know how often selfishness, hurt feelings, and laziness mar our relationships with one another. You know how we are when no one is watching. But we love You, and You are teaching us to love. Increase our love; let it shine out for everyone around to see. Make us a light on a hill, Lord, so that those in darkness would see our Jesus. Amen.

....

....

....

....

Evening
TRUTH SETS YOU FREE

To the Jews who had believed him, Jesus said, "If you hold
to my teaching, you are really my disciples. Then you will
know the truth, and the truth will set you free."

JOHN 8:31–32 NIV

Lord, I am free! For so long I was bound in sin and selfishness. I tried to change, but I was powerless; I could not break free on my own. You loosed the chains that held me. Your love and strength empowered me, Lord. I choose to follow the way of freedom. Your truth sets me free!

....

....

....

....

....

Morning
NO SLIPPING

He will not suffer thy foot to be moved: he that keepeth thee will not slumber.
PSALM 121:3 KJV

I'm coming to a situation in my life where the way ahead looks slippery and dangerous, Lord. Please hold my hand, and when necessary, pick me up and carry me. I know that You won't leave me or even take a break to get a little rest. Thank You that I can rest in You, even during difficult stretches of the path.

....

....

....

....

....

Evening
CHANGE ME, LORD

Yet you, LORD, are our Father. We are the clay,
you are the potter; we are all the work of your hand.
ISAIAH 64:8 NIV

Lord, You know my past, present, and future. You are the potter, and I am the clay, the work of Your hands. As You reshape my life, molding me into the woman You want me to be, help me to trust Your wisdom. I want to be a vessel sturdy enough to hold all the love You have for me—and to pour that out on others.

....

....

....

....

....

Morning
THE REAL ME

I have chosen the way of truth.
PSALM 119:30 NKJV

Heavenly Father, so many people in my world wear masks. We are afraid to be real with others; we fear losing the respect and esteem of our peers. And, oddly enough, we're often afraid to be real with even You—and You know everything about us anyway. I want to be genuine in my approach and interaction with others, including You. Give me the courage to reject the lure of artificial "perfectness" and instead live out my life and relationships in a real way. Amen.

....

....

....

....

Evening
GOD GIVES JOY

For God giveth to a man that is good in
his sight wisdom, and knowledge, and joy.
ECCLESIASTES 2:26 KJV

Oh, Giver of all things good, how grateful I am that You have granted me godly happiness. I am truly undeserving of this blessing, but what refreshment it is to turn from the cares of everyday life and be bathed in Your eternal joy! I am humbled when I recall how willingly You gave of Yourself that I might experience this pleasure.

....

....

....

....

....

Morning

COBWEBS OF THE SOUL

You will keep him in perfect peace, whose mind is stayed on You.
ISAIAH 26:3 NKJV

Dear Father, You know how good I feel when my house is in order. It imparts an order and peace to my soul. And You know how I feel when chaos reigns: scattered, bewildered, short tempered. Help me remember that it is no different with my spiritual house. Help me keep the cobwebs and confusion in check with daily prayer, study, and meditation on Your Word. And thank You that I *can*. Amen.

....

....

....

....

Evening

MOVING PAST MY MISTAKES

"The thief comes only to steal and kill and destroy; I have come that they may have life, and have it to the full."
JOHN 10:10 NIV

God, You don't speak to me according to my past mistakes, and my heavenly rewards are not based on how many times I failed or succeeded. Although I can't erase my past, You can—and have. Thank You for removing my transgressions and filling me with Your great love and kindness in exchange. Help me learn from my past and move forward.

....

....

....

....

....

Morning

STRAIGHT WAYS

*Lead me, O LORD, in thy righteousness because of mine
enemies; make thy way straight before my face.*

PSALM 5:8 KJV

God, You know how hard it is for me sometimes to know which way I should go. Today I ask that You be my map and my Guide. Please show me clearly the way You want me to follow. Remind me that You've already "been there and done that." While I may question why we're going a certain way, You know what is best and have great plans for me.

....

....

....

....

....

Evening

LETTING GO OF THE PAST

My eyes are ever on the LORD, for only he will release my feet from the snare.

PSALM 25:15 NIV

Lord, it's hard to let go of things that are familiar, even when they're not good for me anymore. I need Your strong power to release my grasp, finger by finger, on the things I cling to so tightly—like unhealthy ways of thinking or relationships that are not bearing fruit. As I release them to You, give me the courage to receive all You have waiting for my empty, trusting hands.

....

....

....

....

....

Morning

ACCOUNTABILITY

The LORD will be at your side and will keep your foot from being snared.
PROVERBS 3:26 NIV

Lord, often Christian leaders fall into great sin. Their lives and ministries crumble to bits when sin that was hidden comes to light. Those leaders probably never imagined where their sin would take them, and I thank You for reminding me that I too am capable of any sin. Please protect me, Lord. Surround me with people who will hold me accountable. I want to be useful to You, Lord, not a broken object of scorn and pity. Amen.

....

....

....

....

....

Evening

FRIENDS LIKE JESUS

One who loves purity of heart and whose speech is gracious, the king is his friend.
PROVERBS 22:11 NASB

When my heart is pure and I speak with grace, it's because You are my Friend and show me how to touch the hearts of others. In times of trouble, people have shown me their friendship. Their pure hearts and gracious speech have comforted my soul. Thank You for their love—and thank You most of all that You have been the Friend who stood by me in the blackest times.

....

....

....

....

Morning

PLAIN PATHS

Teach me thy way, O LORD, and lead me
in a plain path, because of mine enemies.

PSALM 27:11 KJV

I need Your help, Lord. I can't see which path I should take. It's dark, I'm confused, and the enemy of my soul has hidden Your way from me. Please, Lord, lead me—and remove the evil that is in the way!

....

....

....

....

....

....

Evening

GOD'S PLANS

"For I know the plans I have for you," declares the LORD, "plans to
prosper you and not to harm you, plans to give you hope and a future."

JEREMIAH 29:11 NIV

When I don't know where to go or how to make the best choices, I need someone to set my path. Lord, You see the big picture and You want to direct me daily in the best way. All I have to do is listen, and the route lies before me. Thank You, Lord, for planning my days and my future.

....

....

....

....

....

Morning
WALKING IN TRUTH

Teach me thy way, O Lord; I will walk in
thy truth: unite my heart to fear thy name.
PSALM 86:11 KJV

I am guilty of having a divided heart, God. I want to do Your will, but I also want my will to be done. Forgive me for my selfishness. When my heart feels torn with conflicting desires, Father God, please unite me so that I have a single focus in life: Your way, Your truth, Your will, Your path.

....

....

....

....

....

Evening
TRUST IN THE SAVIOR

Give your burdens to the Lord, and he will take care of
you. He will not permit the godly to slip and fall.
PSALM 55:22 NLT

Lord, I know nothing happens to me that You do not know about, and You are always looking out for my well-being. Keep my heart firm in this truth, no matter what I face. I want to be firm in faith, trusting only in You, my Savior. Take each of my burdens now, Lord. When Your help is there for me, I don't want to bear them alone.

....

....

....

....

....

Morning

A DREAM DEFERRED CAN BLOOM

He hath made every thing beautiful in his time.

ECCLESIASTES 3:11 KJV

When I feel small and insignificant, Lord, You so graciously remind me of this verse. Thank You for the contentment that only comes from following You. But I thank You too for how You are fulfilling some of my old dreams in unexpected ways. I love You, and I trust You completely. If my heart is set on You, then what You give me *will* be the desire of my heart. Amen.

....

....

....

....

....

Evening

GOD'S WATCHFUL CARE

The LORD watches over the foreigner and sustains the fatherless and the widow, but he frustrates the ways of the wicked.

PSALM 146:9 NIV

Lord, I'm so glad You watch over the weak, the downhearted, and the ones left out by the world. When life feels unfair, it's comforting to know You have not left me. Right now, I feel so powerless, Lord. Help me trust in You for direction for my future. Thank You for caring when I am in trouble. I need Your help right now, Jesus.

....

....

....

....

....

Morning

FRIENDS FOR EVERY NEED

A time to weep, and a time to laugh; a time to mourn, and a time to dance.
ECCLESIASTES 3:4 NKJV

Dear heavenly Father, I am grateful for my friends. They are such a vital part of my life. When I need someone to gripe to, they will listen. When I need a kick to get me going again, they don't hesitate. My journey through life would be so lonely and unhappy without these amazing women who walk it with me. Thank You for blessing me through them. Help me return the favor. Amen.

....

....

....

....

Evening

COVENANT LOVE

*"Therefore know that the LORD your God, He is God, the faithful
God who keeps covenant and mercy for a thousand generations
with those who love Him and keep His commandments."*
DEUTERONOMY 7:9 NKJV

You are so faithful, Lord. Despite my failings, You desired a relationship with me. Even when I have fallen short of Your will and gone against Your Word, You've encouraged me to turn again and keep the commandments You made for my benefit. Your faithfulness awes me, Jesus. Through Your Spirit, I want to stand as firm in all I do.

....

....

....

....

....

Morning
MORNING LOVE

Cause me to hear thy lovingkindness in the morning;
for in thee do I trust: cause me to know the way wherein
I should walk; for I lift up my soul unto thee.

PSALM 143:8 KJV

It is my desire, Father God, to meet You in prayer every morning. As I start out each day, give me ears to hear Your voice. May I listen for that still, small voice all through my day. Follow me into the evening and whisper loving thoughts to me at night as I rest my head, ready to meet You again in the morning.

Evening
ABOUNDING GRACE

And God is able to bless you abundantly, so that in all things at all
times, having all that you need, you will abound in every good work.

2 CORINTHIANS 9:8 NIV

When my hands and heart do the right thing, it's because of Your grace. With Your grace and blessings, I become Your faithful servant whose works glorify Your kingdom. I am blessed by the grace that causes me to abound in good deeds for You and want to share Your love with everyone I know.

Morning
GOD'S EYE

I will instruct thee and teach thee in the way which
thou shalt go: I will guide thee with mine eye.
PSALM 32:8 KJV

I have a dog that follows the direction of my gaze and knows what I want her to do. Lord, help me be as responsive to Your gaze. Keep me so tuned into You that You can use Your eyes to show me where You want me to go.

....

....

....

....

....

Evening
FOREVER MERCY

Surely goodness and mercy shall follow me all the days of my
life: and I will dwell in the house of the LORD for ever.
PSALM 23:6 KJV

Lord, Your goodness and mercy follow me *every* day of my life, not just on happy ones. Though I feel sad, lonely, and doubtful, You still offer me mercy. Help me focus on the eternity You've promised I will spend with You and trust that when earth fades away, I'll find myself in heaven with my merciful Savior. Thank You for Your goodness and mercy.

....

....

....

....

....

....

Morning
A CAGED BIRD SINGING

Rejoice to the extent that you partake of Christ's sufferings, that when
His glory is revealed, you may also be glad with exceeding joy.

1 PETER 4:13 NKJV

Dear God, thank You for Paul and Silas, who prayed and sang hymns from
their jail cell. Your Word says the other prisoners were *listening* to them,
learning what it means to serve a risen Savior. Nothing like that has ever
happened to me, Lord, and I am very grateful. But I pray that even still,
I would be faithful to praise You—because people are listening. Amen.

....

....

....

....

....

Evening
GOD BESIDE ME

But you are near, O LORD, and all your commands are true.

PSALM 119:151 NLT

Thank You, Lord, for being near to me even when trouble stands on my
other side. Thank You for this double promise that You always stay by me
and never change Your truths. Your faithfulness in all my trials deserves all
my praise, Lord. No one stands by me like You. There's nothing You won't
do for me as long as I'm faithful too. Help me walk with You, following
Your commands all my days.

....

....

....

....

Morning

MOVING AND MAKING FRIENDS

A man who has friends must himself be friendly.
PROVERBS 18:24 NKJV

God, I don't like change. I'd rather stay in my comfort zone, but here I am in a new environment. I miss my old friends so much. I feel like crying just thinking about them. But that won't do any good, will it? I need some heavenly moxie. It's time to square my shoulders, walk in, smile, introduce myself, and meet some new people. I guess I can think of them as pre-friends. Help me avoid chickening out! Thank You. Amen.

....

....

....

....

Evening

BEFORE BIRTH

Your eyes saw my substance, being yet unformed. And in Your book they all were written, the days fashioned for me, when as yet there were none of them.
PSALM 139:16 NKJV

Even before I was born, You knew just what every day of my life would be like, Jesus. I can barely take this truth in! Though I may face days that seem out of control, I need to remind myself I need not worry. Nothing in this life is beyond Your authority. Your greatness humbles me, Lord. Beyond all things, I want to glorify You.

....

....

....

....

....

Morning
FOR MY OWN GOOD

Thus saith the LORD, thy Redeemer, the Holy One of Israel;
I am the LORD thy God which teacheth thee to profit, which
leadeth thee by the way that thou shouldest go.

ISAIAH 48:17 KJV

Sometimes I forget, Lord, that Your guidance is always for my good. I admit that sometimes it feels a little bit like taking my medicine. But You want what's truly best for me. Your paths always lead me to joy and blessing and health. Teach me to trust You more fully today and every day.

....

....

....

....

Evening
ANGER

Get rid of all bitterness, rage and anger, brawling
and slander, along with every form of malice.

EPHESIANS 4:31 NIV

Lord, I am angry and I need Your help. I need to do something with this heated emotion—and I choose to give You my anger and bitterness, Lord. Help me be rid of it. Redeem the confusion and bring peace to what seems so out of control. Free me from resentment and blame. Show me my part in this conflict as You speak to the heart of my nemesis. I need Your healing and peace, Lord.

....

....

....

....

....

Morning
OPEN EARS

And thine ears shall hear a word behind thee, saying,
This is the way, walk ye in it, when ye turn
to the right hand, and when ye turn to the left.
ISAIAH 30:21 KJV

Give me sharp ears, heavenly Father, so that I can hear Your voice. Tune my ears to be receptive only to You, and give me discernment so I can disregard the false voices that may try to imitate You.

....

....

....

....

....

Evening
FUTURE JOY

Weeping may last through the night, but joy comes with the morning.
PSALM 30:5 NLT

Lord, You encourage me to believe my sorrow will not last forever. While I can't imagine joy, You look out for my future, preparing good things. When I cannot look ahead, You do it for me. I can't thank You enough, Jesus, for watching over me. Thank You for putting joy in my future. One morning, it will flood my soul.

....

....

....

....

....

....

Morning
THE PROOF IS IN THE PUDDING

"Then you will know the truth, and the truth will set you free."
JOHN 8:32 NIV

Dear Father, from the very beginning, we were tricked and led astray. Satan whispered in Eve's ear, she listened, and everyone ever since has been falling for his lies. We believe his lies about so many things. I need You every moment, Lord, to help me sort through the chatter in my head so I can be certain what to listen to and what to stand against. Only the truth. Only what glorifies You. Amen.

....

....

....

....

....

Evening
BLESSINGS

"But blessed is the one who trusts in the LORD, whose confidence is in him."
JEREMIAH 17:7 NIV

My confidence lies in my Creator, who controls all things in heaven and earth. My situation looks small and simple to You, and nothing I face surprises You. Thank You for giving me this promise to hold on to when my faith weakens. Though I may not see it yet, You *are* blessing me. Help me continue to trust that all my ways will be redeemed as I hold on to You.

....

....

....

....

....

Morning
DELIGHTED LOVE

No, the LORD's delight is in those who fear him,
those who put their hope in his unfailing love.
PSALM 147:11 NLT

You delight in me, Lord. How wonderful that the Lord of heaven and earth loves me this way. As I treasure Your love, may I also never take it for granted. I want to honor You and bring You joy daily. Knowing You never fail me should make that easy, yet sin still invades my best intentions. Keep me mindful of Your faithfulness to me so I can be faithful to You too.

....

....

....

....

....

Evening
RECONCILIATION

Be kind to each other, tenderhearted, forgiving one
another, just as God through Christ has forgiven you.
EPHESIANS 4:32 NLT

Dear Lord, I just can't believe that my friend and I had this disagreement. It feels so odd to have a chill between us instead of the warm camaraderie we've always shared. I'm still hurt over what she said. Maybe she feels the same about the words that came out of my mouth. Please help us both take steps toward reconciliation. What do You want me to do right now to start repairing this friendship? Amen.

....

....

....

....

Morning
NO MORE CROOKED WAYS

I will bring the blind by a way that they knew not; I will lead them in paths that they have not known: I will make darkness light before them, and crooked things straight. These things will I do unto them, and not forsake them.

ISAIAH 42:16 KJV

Sometimes my life seems to take one unexpected turn after another. I feel like I'm stumbling through a dark maze. One day, though, Lord, when I look back at my life from heaven's perspective, will I see that You made my life's crooked paths run absolutely straight, right to You?

....

....

....

....

Evening
CHANGELESS LORD

The LORD is gracious and full of compassion, slow to anger and great in mercy.

PSALM 145:8 NKJV

When grief overwhelms me, it's easy to start questioning You, Lord. *How could this happen?* I wonder, and it doesn't take long for me to start wondering about Your goodness. You remind me that though my circumstances have changed, Your eternal goodness cannot. No matter how I'm feeling, Your graciousness, compassion, forgiveness, and mercy work in my life. Turn aside the doubts that would separate us, Jesus. I want to be faithful to You, no matter how I feel today.

....

....

....

....

....

Morning

LITTLE MARY QUITE EXTRAORDINARY

"For He who is mighty has done great things for me, and holy is His name."
LUKE 1:49 NKJV

God, thank You so much for Mary, this girl who became the mother of God. I thank You for her amazing example of humility and exuberant praise. Everything she said glorified You. She found favor in Your eyes and became a witness to the Incarnation, the defining event of history. You delight in turning our expectations on their head this way! Help me be more like Mary and say continually, "Let it be to me according to Your word." Amen.

....

....

....

....

Evening

TO UNDERSTAND THE BIBLE

You made me and formed me with your hands.
Give me understanding so I can learn your commands.
PSALM 119:73 NCV

The Bible is Your Word for my life. Help me understand what You are saying to me through it. Give me wisdom and understanding as I allow scripture to feed my spirit and fill me with Your strength. I read Your words so I can grow and learn more about You. Bring the words I read back to mind when I need to apply them to the circumstances I face.

....

....

....

....

....

Morning

THE PATH OF LIFE

Thou wilt shew me the path of life: in thy presence is fulness
of joy; at thy right hand there are pleasures for evermore.

PSALM 16:11 KJV

Why do I think I'm a trailblazer, Lord? Sometimes my way seems better
to me, so I take a little side trip off Your path, only to find disappointment,
destruction, and heartbreak. I know that only Your path, God, leads me
to life. . .to joy. . .to pleasures that will last forever. I will put blinders on
my eyes, Father—looking straight ahead to You.

....

....

....

....

Evening

FAITHFUL IN TRIALS

"Yahweh! The LORD! The God of compassion and mercy! I am
slow to anger and filled with unfailing love and faithfulness."

EXODUS 34:6 NLT

When life becomes challenging, I'm tempted to think the world has gone
awry and wickedness has won. It's not true, of course. This promise of Your
nature, so large and unfailing in love, has never been destroyed. Though trials
come, keep me mindful of Your unchanging mercy and graciousness, poured
out even in the worst situations. Help me see Your work, Jesus, in everything.

....

....

....

....

....

Morning
LIFTING WEIGHTS OF SIN

"Forgive, and you will be forgiven."
LUKE 6:37 NIV

Dear Lord, I am struggling to forgive. Each time I do this, Lord—allow You to come into a situation and help me forgive—it feels like the hardest thing I have ever done. I lay my burden at the cross, and suddenly I feel lighter. But then I walk over and pick it up again. I am looking to You, Jesus. Help me carry my cross daily in forgiveness and follow You. Amen.

....

....

....

....

....

Evening
ENDURING LOVE

Give thanks to the God of gods. His faithful love endures forever.
PSALM 136:2 NLT

Nothing can stop Your faithful love, because no one and nothing is greater than You. If Your touch seems distant, help me trust in You, turning from sin to faith. Thanks should fill my life as I rely on Your love. Keep me faithful and thankful in all my trials, Lord. Help me cling to Your powerful love and draw near to You. Nothing else will fill my heart with joy. Thank You, Lord, for Your unending love.

....

....

....

....

....

Morning
STANDING UP STRAIGHT

Teach me to do thy will; for thou art my God:
thy spirit is good; lead me into the land of uprightness.

PSALM 143:10 KJV

My burdens have been feeling extra heavy lately, Father. I am still walking along Your path, but maybe You've noticed my shoulders slumped, my head hung low. Gently remind me that I don't need to carry these burdens—that You are strong enough to carry all the weight of the world. I give You my worries and woes, Father. Help me stand upright and follow the path of Your perfect will.

....

....

....

....

Evening
GLAD LIFE

The humble shall see [God's salvation] and be glad;
and you who seek God, your hearts shall live.

PSALM 69:32 NKJV

I felt Your touch, Jesus, and joy filled my heart. You never meant that delight to fade. Your joy should be an everlasting theme in my daily living. Trials often begin to squeeze gladness from my life. Trouble doesn't have to rule my days. Thank You for the promise, Lord, that if I humbly turn and draw closer to You, joy will reignite. Draw me near today. Your new life fills my heart, even in troublesome times.

....

....

....

....

Morning

MENTORING

*That [the aged women] may teach the young women to
be sober, to love their husbands, to love their children.*

TITUS 2:4 KJV

Dear God, the Bible tells older women to mentor younger women. Lord, I need a trusted confidante, one who will help me succeed. I ask You to send someone like that my way in fulfillment of Your Word. And let me fill that role myself someday when I have the required résumé. Amen.

....

....

....

....

....

Evening

ETERNAL LIFE

*"And as Moses lifted up the serpent in the wilderness, even
so must the Son of Man be lifted up, that whoever believes
in Him should not perish but have eternal life."*

JOHN 3:14–15 NKJV

Your sacrifice, Jesus, made my new life possible. Help me live each day aware of the price You paid. You work out Your life in me each day, through troubles and joys. No matter what discouragement I face, You still achieve Your eternal purpose. I seek eternity each day, Lord, trusting that one day, I'll share unending bliss with You.

....

....

....

....

Morning
EVERLASTING WAYS

See if there be any wicked way in me, and lead me in the way everlasting.
PSALM 139:24 KJV

You know, Lord God, how easily I hide selfishness inside my heart. But try as I might, I cannot hide it from You. Shine Your light on all my blind spots. Show me where I need to grow and change to be more like You. Bring true godly friends into my life that can help me in these areas. Lead me in the path that will lead me to eternity.

....

....

....

....

....

Evening
PATIENCE'S END

Better is the end of a thing than the beginning of it,
and the patient in spirit is better than the proud in spirit.
ECCLESIASTES 7:8 AMPC

Lord, pride lands me in trouble, while patience paves the way for good things. I have to admit I'm not very patient. Especially when I'm under pressure, I want things now and I want people to do things my way. When Your Spirit controls my life, I relax, accept another way, and live in Your peace. No matter what trials I face today, make me patient, Lord.

....

....

....

....

....

Morning
INSTRUCTIONS IN RIGHTEOUSNESS

"But I tell you, love your enemies and pray for those who persecute you, that you may be children of your Father in heaven."
MATTHEW 5:44–45 NIV

Lord, thank You for this verse. I can't hold on to my negative feelings about a person when I'm lifting them up to You. When I obey your powerful Word, I feel Your power at work in me. When I feel crushed by the weight of unforgiveness, this verse gives me a specific prayer to pray and tells what will happen if I do. Thank You for showing me how. Amen.

....
....
....
....

Evening
IN CONTROL

But the LORD's plans stand firm forever;
his intentions can never be shaken.
PSALM 33:11 NLT

It's hard to imagine that Your intentions are immutable, Lord. But I'm glad nothing alters with You, because I need a Rock to stand firm on. It's good to know You have a blueprint for life that nothing can overthrow. I may not see Your design, but Your strategy still leads my out-of-control life to victory. As You direct a life, it always comes to perfect completion. Jesus, thank You for Your unchanging love.

....
....
....
....
....

Morning

THE SAME OLD ME

You have searched me, LORD, and you know me.
PSALM 139:1 NIV

Lord, today I come to You a bit discouraged. It seems I could do much more for You without some of the inherent flaws of my personality. So help me overcome my defects, or use me in spite of them. Help me love myself and strive to be the best me I can be. I know You can find a way to use me for Your glory. Amen.

....

....

....

....

....

Evening

REST ASSURED

"Be still, and know that I am God; I will be exalted among the nations, I will be exalted in the earth."
PSALM 46:10 NIV

Lord, thank You for the gift of Your peace and contentment in my life. You are awesome! I am learning that I can be at peace because You have a plan. You can handle anything—my entire life. You are sovereign, powerful, and wise—and You never drop the ball. Because of who You are, I can be still and rest assured, confident no matter what comes my way. Thank You, Lord.

....

....

....

....

....

Morning
FUTURE GLORY

*For I reckon that the sufferings of this present time are not worthy
to be compared with the glory which shall be revealed in us.*
ROMANS 8:18 KJV

When it comes down to it, God, it's not all about me. I am guilty of being so selfish, self-centered, "me focused" that I lose perspective of the big picture. Father God, when pain surrounds me, give me a glimpse of the glory that lies ahead. Help me regain a proper sense of perspective. Show me where You want me in Your will!

....

....

....

....

....

Evening
PEACE WITH OTHERS

Live in peace with each other.
1 THESSALONIANS 5:13 NIV

Lord, I need Your peace today. Some people are just hard to be around. They talk too much or are too needy. Our personalities rub each other the wrong way. God, I need the power of Your Holy Spirit to stay calm. I don't want to be frustrated or lose my temper. I want to be at peace around others—even the people who differ from me. Impart in me Your loving ways so I can be at peace with others.

....

....

....

....

Morning
ETERNAL

For our light affliction, which is but for a moment, worketh
for us a far more exceeding and eternal weight of glory.

2 CORINTHIANS 4:17 KJV

When I think about eternity, God, I realize that the time I spend on earth is pretty insignificant. But I still get so focused on my daily problems, Lord, that they seem insurmountable. Burdens and worries eat away at my joy, Lord. Instead, I choose to yield myself to whatever comes into my life and rely on Your power to get me through. Use my problems and troubles to transform me for eternity.

....

....

....

....

Evening
FINDING CONTENTMENT

But godliness with contentment is great gain.

1 TIMOTHY 6:6 NIV

Lord, please help me find my contentment in You. I don't want to be defined by "stuff"—the things I own or what I do. May my greatest happiness in life be knowing who You are and who I am in Christ. May I treasure the simple things in life, those things that bring me peace. With Your grace, I rest secure. Like Mary, I choose to sit at Your feet. You, Lord, are my satisfaction.

....

....

....

....

....

Morning
FORGIVE

You are from God, little children, and have overcome them;
because greater is He who is in you than he who is in the world.

1 JOHN 4:4 NASB

Lord, I am so slow to learn Your lessons. But You are patient and loving. . .
and *long-suffering*. Thank You for not giving up on me as I learn to forgive. I
remember the first time You helped me win this battle. I felt Your joy flood
my heart. And I was *stronger*. Help me remember this victory, Lord, and keep
strengthening my muscles for the harder battles to come. Amen.

....

....

....

....

....

Evening
MANAGING YOUR HOUSEHOLD

She watches over the affairs of her household
and does not eat the bread of idleness.

PROVERBS 31:27 NIV

Lord, thank You for the wisdom you give me to watch over the affairs of my
household. Give me energy to accomplish my work and to keep our home
running smoothly. Help me be a good time manager and stay centered on
Your purposes. I need to get my tasks done, but I also want to nurture and
cherish my relationships. Empower me, Lord. Help our home be a place
of order, peace, and enjoyment.

....

....

....

....

Morning
GOD'S PURPOSE

You can make many plans, but the LORD's purpose will prevail.
PROVERBS 19:21 NLT

Lord, the future seems unpredictable because my mind is overwhelmed. At this moment, I put all my strategies in Your hands. Take control of everything I do and say. Show me Your purpose in my life or guide me in the right direction, even though I cannot understand. I need Your design to guide my days because I want Your purpose to prevail. Achieve Your goals in my life, Lord.

....

....

....

....

Evening
NOT GOOD ENOUGH

I praise you because I am fearfully and wonderfully made.
PSALM 139:14 NIV

Father, shopping for clothing at the mall makes me so insecure. The store windows are filled with posters of glamorous women. Like every other woman I know, I struggle with body image. Although these feelings of inferiority seem petty, they are so real sometimes that I get depressed. I know that isn't what You want for me. Help me with these feelings, and show me the way to triumph over them. In Christ's name, amen.

....

....

....

....

....

Morning

BLESSED HOPE

*Looking for that blessed hope, and the glorious appearing
of the great God and our Saviour Jesus Christ.*

TITUS 2:13 KJV

Some days, Father, I hold on to a single thread of hope. But the hope You offer through Jesus Christ is real and active, and even when it's wearing thin, it sustains me. The hope I have in You, God, is for the future—but it blesses me today. Fortify my hope so that I can share it with other weary travelers in this world. Help me direct them to the true source of hope.

....

....

....

....

Evening

A FAMILY THAT PRAYS TOGETHER

*He and all his family were devout and God-fearing; he gave
generously to those in need and prayed to God regularly.*

ACTS 10:2 NIV

Lord, I want our family to pray together more often. We need to put You first because You are the source of life—and You are worthy of our time. Help us make spending time with You a priority. I pray that meeting with You together will draw us closer to You and to one another. I ask for Your blessing as we seek to honor You in this way.

....

....

....

....

....

Morning

WHEN CHRIST APPEARS

When Christ, who is our life, shall appear,
then shall ye also appear with him in glory.
COLOSSIANS 3:4 KJV

Jesus, I look forward to Your return to earth. I'm so thankful that I am not on my own—that You are with me all the way. Thank You for the gift of Your Holy Spirit that lives in me and empowers me with the strength necessary to live for God. You are my life now, and You will take me with You into glory, where I will be made perfect.

....

....

....

....

Evening

SERVE THE LORD

"But if serving the LORD seems undesirable to you,
then choose for yourselves this day whom you will serve. . . .
But as for me and my household, we will serve the LORD."
JOSHUA 24:15 NIV

Lord, this world offers so many choices of things or people to whom we could give our allegiance. Please give me the strength to serve You. As I humbly bow before You, I ask that You would provide for my needs—so I can help supply the needs of others through my service and hospitality.

....

....

....

....

....

Morning
THE POWER OF WORDS

Death and life are in the power of the tongue:
and they that love it shall eat the fruit thereof.
PROVERBS 18:21 KJV

Father, keep me aware of my words. Let me apologize if I've hurt anyone. Better yet, let me consider my words before I cast them out on the wind. Your Word is living, brilliant, and powerful; Jesus is the Living Word. My words are weighty as well; they can minister life or death to those who hear. I ask You to remind me of this throughout the day. Amen.

....

....

....

....

Evening
RENEWING YOUR MIND

Do not conform to the pattern of this world, but be transformed
by the renewing of your mind. Then you will be able to test and
approve what God's will is—his good, pleasing and perfect will.
ROMANS 12:2 NIV

Lord, sometimes my emotions need a makeover. Renovate me—transform me so my emotions are balanced and healthy. I ask for your power to change. I want to be wise and enjoy sound thinking. I want to make good decisions in how I express myself. Help me know Your will and have a renewed mind.

....

....

....

....

....

Morning

GOD'S THOUGHTS

For I know the thoughts that I think toward you, saith the LORD,
thoughts of peace, and not of evil, to give you an expected end.

JEREMIAH 29:11 KJV

God, You know how easily my thoughts turn to worries and fears. Teach me to think Your thoughts instead: thoughts of peace and goodness that will lead me into the future You have planned for me. Show me the steps I should take to reach the abundant life You have in store for me, both here on earth and in eternity.

....

....

....

....

....

Evening

TRANSFORMING MY THOUGHTS

May the words of my mouth and the meditation of my heart
be pleasing to you, O LORD, my rock and my redeemer.

PSALM 19:14 NLT

Father, Your Word says I can choose what to think about. Help me refuse thoughts that keep me prisoner to things in my past or to worries about my future. My hope is in You. You are my strength and my shield. Transform my thoughts with the truth of Your Word. When I read the Bible, help me remember Your Word. Then when my mind wanders to matters that bring me down, I will recall what You have to say about them.

....

....

....

....

Morning
THE PEBBLE

*"You did not choose me, but I chose you and appointed you
so that you might go and bear fruit—fruit that will last."*
JOHN 15:16 NIV

Sometimes I feel like I have no influence, Lord. Yet You comfort and empower me with Your Word, again. Thank You for reminding me that no matter what small circles we move in, we are all leaders to someone: a child, a wife, a younger brother, a shy new believer in church. I am a tiny pebble thrown into the sea, Lord, but my ripples will travel. Amen.

....

....

....

....

....

Evening
HIS RESCUE

*"Because he loves me," says the LORD, "I will rescue him;
I will protect him, for he acknowledges my name."*
PSALM 91:14 NIV

Those who love You are rescued by You, Jesus! What a wonderful promise. You have sent me unexpected help before I could even ask. Thank You for Your faithful love. Now I need Your rescue from suffering, faithful Lord. Though my situation may not change, You can make a change in me. Work in my life, complete Your process of reclamation, and make me holy in You.

....

....

....

....

Morning
BEFORE THE WORLD BEGAN

*In hope of eternal life, which God, that cannot
lie, promised before the world began.*
TITUS 1:2 KJV

Think of it, Father! You are a God that cannot lie—there is no falsehood or deceit in You. Your promises are better than gold and they reach forward into eternity—and they reach backward, before the heavens and earth were made. There is no place in time's long arc where You are not, so why should I worry about past, present, or future? Hold me in Your hand today.

....

....

....

....

....

Evening
LIVING WITH PAIN

Great is the LORD and most worthy of praise; his greatness no one can fathom.
PSALM 145:3 NIV

Lord, I choose to praise You through this pain. You are great, and there is no one worthy of Your honor and glory. I give You this discomfort and ask in the name and power of Jesus that You would take it away. Help me, and heal me completely from my hurt. Let my heart ache only for the comfort and healing balm of Your presence.

....

....

....

....

....

Morning

GOD'S RICHES

Oh, the depth of the riches, both of the wisdom and knowledge of God!
How unsearchable are His judgments and unfathomable His ways!
ROMANS 11:33 NASB

When I start to worry about my life, Father, when I start to feel as though
You may not know what You're doing—remind me that Your riches are far
greater than my needs. Give me a spirit of peace when I don't understand
the whys, secure in my faith that You are doing a good work that will bring
glory to Your name.

....

....

....

....

....

Evening

FRUIT OF THE SPIRIT

But the fruit of the Spirit is love, joy, peace, longsuffering, gentleness,
goodness, faith, meekness, temperance: against such there is no law.
GALATIANS 5:22–23 KJV

I don't see how I could be Your child and not have joy in my life, dear God.
You are at work in my soul. You will cultivate joy within me if I will let
You. Then others will see it. Please let the soil of my heart be fertile for the
seeds You want to sow.

....

....

....

....

....

Morning
THE MISSING LINK

*Then God said, "Let there be light"; and there was light. God saw that
the light was good; and God separated the light from the darkness.*
GENESIS 1:3–4 NASB

Dear Lord, sometimes I have to laugh at how hard people work to explain
life apart from a Creator. Thank You for creating the universe out of nothing
and us out of the dust of the earth. You spoke light into existence. We could
never design a universe so complex, detailed, and interlocking. Thank You
for the amazing love that keeps it all spinning. Amen.

....

....

....

....

Evening
NEW FRIENDS

*If one falls down, the other can help him up. But it is bad for the
person who is alone and falls, because no one is there to help.*
ECCLESIASTES 4:10 NCV

Lord, there are people out there who are hard to love. Help me look beyond
their negative attributes. You love every one of us. If we were friends even
to our enemies, the world would be at peace. No one deserves to be alone.
Give me the courage and strength to reach out to all people and to make
new friends.

....

....

....

....

....

Morning
ALL GRACE

The God of all grace, who hath called us unto his eternal
glory by Christ Jesus, after that ye have suffered a while,
make you perfect, stablish, strengthen, settle you.
1 PETER 5:10 KJV

I'm glad, God, that Your grace is so wide and great that it can work even through this life's pain and suffering. Give me the right amount of comfort to endure those times of pain and suffering, and remind me that in the end, I can count on You to make me perfect and strong, settled in Your love forever.

....

....

....

....

....

Evening
GIVING GOD CONTROL OF MY FUTURE

People may make plans in their minds, but the LORD decides what they will do.
PROVERBS 16:9 NCV

Jesus, You knew that God's will was for You to give Your life so that others may experience God. You gave God total control and submitted to His will. Help me do the same. I was created for a specific purpose. You have a plan for my life, and I want to complete everything You created me to accomplish. Help me live my life according to Your ultimate plan.

....

....

....

....

....

Morning
ABUNDANCE

*[God] is able to do exceeding abundantly above all that we
ask or think, according to the power that worketh in us.*
EPHESIANS 3:20 KJV

Father, I often put limits on what is possible in my life. Help me recall
the miracles You've done in my life—the incidents that have Your finger-
prints all over them. Help me share these fantastic stories with others
so they too might learn to see You at work in their lives. Give me Your
eyes to see the endless power You have at work in me. May I expect Your
abundance to fill my future.

....

....

....

....

Evening
JUSTICE IN JESUS

He guards the paths of the just and protects those who are faithful to him.
PROVERBS 2:8 NLT

Lord, I can count on Your promise to guard and protect me because I've
been faithful to You. It doesn't always seem like that when I'm in the middle
of a trial. Help me trust in You, even when justice seems distant. Keep me
faithful to You, no matter what situation lies before me. Thank You for
bringing good even out of my troubles. I trust in You for all things.

....

....

....

....

....

Morning
OBSIDIAN

*The LORD liveth; and blessed be my rock; and
exalted be the God of the rock of my salvation.*
2 SAMUEL 22:47 KJV

Lord, today I praise You with a kind of wide-eyed joy. I feel patience
thickening like a skin over the lava of my usual anger, and I know that it
can only come from You. I walk gingerly, Lord, because I don't yet trust
myself. Will I fall through? Is it thick enough to hold? But thank You for
what You are slowly forming beneath my feet: solid rock. Amen.

....

....

....

....

Evening
RESTORING A BROKEN FRIENDSHIP

Above all, love each other deeply, because love covers over a multitude of sins.
1 PETER 4:8 NIV

Lord, I thank You for Your healing balm that covers the hurt and pain I've
experienced in this friendship. Your grace covers me, Your love repairs my
brokenness, and You give me the ability to love again. Help me put aside
the wounds of my heart and be a friend again. I thank You and praise You
that Your love is healing and restoring. Thank You, Lord, for putting this
friendship back together again.

....

....

....

....

....

Morning

NO SPIRIT OF FEAR

For God hath not given us the spirit of fear;
but of power, and of love, and of a sound mind.

2 TIMOTHY 1:7 KJV

Father, I deal with a phobia. It isn't anything life threatening, but it's embarrassing. I haven't told anyone, and I'm hoping I never have to. But I ask You now to help me; I don't want my phobia to keep me from living the life You've planned for me. Help me bring this fear to You; show me that You are in control, that You are the security system in my life. I ask this in Jesus' name, amen.

....

....

....

....

Evening

SAVING AND INVESTING

The wise store up choice food and olive oil, but fools gulp theirs down.

PROVERBS 21:20 NIV

Lord, I pray that You would lead me to wise financial advice. When I look, help me find a trusted source who can give me direction as to where to best save and invest my resources. Please provide for my needs today, and help me save for the future. Help me be responsible with my finances as I trust You as my Provider.

....

....

....

....

....

Morning
SHINING MORE AND MORE

The path of the just is as the shining light,
that shineth more and more unto the perfect day.

PROVERBS 4:18 KJV

Father, when I am in vibrant fellowship with You, the path before me seems clearer and Your will seems more evident. Thank You for the light that shines brighter with each step I take. When the light seems dim or I'm not sure which way to go, bring me back into Your presence and lead me to Your holy Word. Thank You for never giving up on me, Father.

....

....

....

....

....

Evening
A RIGHT PERSPECTIVE

We are the temple of the living God. As God has said: "I will live with them
and walk among them, and I will be their God, and they will be my people."

2 CORINTHIANS 6:16 NIV

Father, sometimes I wish I looked different. Remind me that I am wonderfully made by Your hand. Help me be thankful for how You designed me. I want to be a good steward of the body You gave me. Help me nurture, respect, and celebrate it. My body belongs to You! What I do with it reflects on You.

....

....

....

....

....

Morning

PACK NOTHING BUT FAITH

Now faith is the certainty of things hoped for, a proof of things not seen.
HEBREWS 11:1 NASB

Dear Lord, Your world is so beautiful and *large*. Sometimes I sigh for all the places I will never see before I die. I miss them, somehow, though I've never seen them. But I know that nothing good will be lost, and I am confident that in heaven I will ache for nothing left behind. I praise You for what *is* and for what will be. Amen.

....

....

....

....

....

Evening

A MATTER OF SIGNIFICANCE

To them God willed to make known what are the riches of the glory of this mystery among the Gentiles: which is Christ in you, the hope of glory.
COLOSSIANS 1:27 NKJV

Jesus, help me find my identity in You. I know that my relationship with You is significant. As I read the Bible, give me an understanding of who You created me to be. Point out the true identity that has been given to me through the gift of salvation and my relationship with You.

....

....

....

....

....

....

Morning
FIXING MY THOUGHTS

*Fix your thoughts on what is true, and honorable,
and right, and pure, and lovely, and admirable.*
PHILIPPIANS 4:8 NLT

God, today I'm having a pity party. My thoughts are so focused on earthly things that I am having trouble looking up. Lord, You can't work through me when I'm feeling sorry for myself. Forgive me for my pettiness, and let me respond to life with maturity. Help me focus on good, praiseworthy things. In Christ's name, amen.

Evening
SADNESS

*Why, my soul, are you downcast? Why so disturbed within
me? Put your hope in God, for I will yet praise him.*
PSALM 42:5 NIV

Lord, do You see my tears? In my sadness, help me remember that even when I'm down, I can choose to put my hope in You. Instead of telling myself lies that push me deeper into despair, I can look to Your truth. Remind me of the good things You have done in the past. I choose to praise You. You are my Savior. May Your love comfort me now.

Morning

LIKE JESUS

Beloved, now are we the sons of God, and it doth not yet appear what we shall be: but we know that, when he shall appear, we shall be like him; for we shall see him as he is.

1 JOHN 3:2 KJV

God, You promise that You're not done with me yet. In fact, I won't be finished until You come again to the earth and take me home with You. It doesn't really matter what my future holds, God, so long as one day I will be like Jesus.

Evening

GOD'S SHELTERING ARMS

The LORD is a refuge for the oppressed, a stronghold in times of trouble.

PSALM 9:9 NIV

I always need Your shelter from life's storms, Lord. When hurts go deep, I need a place of understanding and love. Thank You, Jesus, for sheltering me when the world seeks to wring all joy from my life. As Your love lives within me wherever I go, Your shelter remains with me, guarding my heart in You. You are the only protection I need.

Morning
FACE-TO-FACE

For now we see through a glass, darkly; but then face to face: now
I know in part; but then shall I know even as also I am known.

1 CORINTHIANS 13:12 KJV

You know that I can't see You clearly, Father. You know I don't really understand You, even when I am seeking You every day. I'm grateful, though, that I expect to see You face-to-face—and that on that day, I will finally truly know You even more intimately and personally than now. What an awe-inspiring promise!

....

....

....

....

....

Evening
CHRIST CAN SAVE

Wherefore he is able also to save them to the uttermost that come unto
God by him, seeing he ever liveth to make intercession for them.

HEBREWS 7:25 KJV

I've known a lot of bad people, Jesus. Although I don't embrace their lifestyles, I can show them Your love. It isn't my place to decide who is worthy of Your grace. I must share You with everyone I meet. Help me be an example to those around me of the truth that Your salvation is for all who come to You.

....

....

....

....

....

Morning

FADELESS BEAUTY

The unfading beauty of a gentle and quiet spirit, which is so precious to God.
1 PETER 3:4 NLT

Dear God, I'm getting older. My body is revolting and my hormones are rebelling. I don't like looking in the mirror because it shocks me to see lines on my face. Inside, I don't feel old, but my body doesn't agree. Lord, help me remember that my identity in You is changeless and my beauty in You is fadeless. I know that in Your sight I have a loveliness that time can't touch. Amen.

....

....

....

....

....

Evening

AN IMITATOR OF GOD

Everyone who believes that Jesus is the Christ has become a child of God.
1 JOHN 5:1 NLT

Father, my relationship with You affects my personality in amazing ways. Forgive me when I've failed to be like You. I want to be so full of Your presence that others see You in everything I say and do. I never want anything I do to reflect negatively on You. I want to be like Jesus, of whom people said, "This truly was the Son of God!"

....

....

....

....

....

Morning

GLORY TO GLORY

*But we all, with open face beholding as in a glass the
glory of the Lord, are changed into the same image
from glory to glory, even as by the Spirit of the Lord.*

2 CORINTHIANS 3:18 KJV

You have given me glory in this world, God. You have given me splendor
and light. You have created my very essence so that it shines. And as I keep
my eyes on You, You are creating within me even greater glory. May Your
Spirit work in my heart, God, so that I am transformed into Your image.

....

....

....

....

Evening

SING WITH GLADNESS

*Therefore the redeemed of the LORD shall return, and come with singing
unto Zion; and everlasting joy shall be upon their head: they shall
obtain gladness and joy; and sorrow and mourning shall flee away.*

ISAIAH 51:11 KJV

Death has no claim on me, for in You I have my victory. One day I will leave
the trials of this world behind and enter the gates of heaven. Oh, what a
day that will be! What joy to know my loved ones will join me as we meet
those who've gone before us. A great day is coming!

....

....

....

....

....

Morning

UNBLEMISHED

And He who sits on the throne said, "Behold, I am making all things new."
REVELATION 21:5 NASB

Lord, I praise You today for babies, for the gift of new life and the new life I have in You. Do You see me this way, Lord? Do I bring You this much joy? Sometimes I have a hard time believing that I—with my sags and bags and scars—am fearfully and wonderfully made. But I trust Your promises and Your love. I trust the blood of Jesus that has washed me into new life. Amen.

....

....

....

....

....

Evening

FAITHFUL PROMISES

Every word of God is pure; He is a shield to those who put their trust in Him.
PROVERBS 30:5 NKJV

You don't make unsubstantiated promises, Lord. I know that. So when You say You'll be my shield because I've trusted in You, I can take You at Your word. I trust You, Lord, to provide all the help I need whenever I face trouble. Be near me, no matter what I experience. Whatever You give me, it will be right.

....

....

....

....

....

....

Morning
STRENGTH TO STRENGTH

They go from strength to strength.
PSALM 84:7 KJV

You know the strength I need to face today, Lord. You know the strength I'll need for tomorrow, for next week, for next year. You know what I'll need to face each of the challenges that lie ahead in my life. You know the day of my death, and You know exactly what I'll need on that day too. So I need not worry about anything. You will lead me from strength to strength, like jumping from stone to stone across a river.

....

....

....

....

Evening
DEAL WITH ANGER

*"In your anger do not sin": Do not let the
sun go down while you are still angry.*
EPHESIANS 4:26 NIV

Lord, I need Your help in dealing with my anger, whether I am simply annoyed, a little mad, or downright furious. I want to handle this feeling in healthy ways. Help me process my emotions and not let them fester inside me. Help me control my temper and talk about what bothers me in calmer ways. Show me how to give my anger to You so I can live in peace.

....

....

....

....

....

Morning

CALM MY HEART

God has not given us a spirit of timidity, but of power and love and discipline.
2 TIMOTHY 1:7 NASB

Lord, rid me of the fears that are plaguing me as I come to You this morning. Calm my racing heart. Fill me with Your strength and courage. The storms feel as if they are going to overcome me, but You have overcome the world and will not let me be brought down. You have given me the spirit of power, love, and self-discipline, and I revel in this knowledge. I praise Your saving name!

....

....

....

....

Evening

WHAT WILL BE

The earth will be full of the knowledge of the LORD as the waters cover the sea.
ISAIAH 11:9 NASB

Father, the more I know about Your creation, the more I marvel at the mind that conceived it. Your creation is irreducibly complex, multifaceted, and breathtakingly beautiful. We are only just beginning to fathom its mysteries. I praise You for the spirit of inquiry that You fashioned in us along with the breath of life. I praise You that You are knowable. I praise You for the day when we will know You fully. Amen.

....

....

....

....

....

Morning
COVETING

Let your conduct be without covetousness.
HEBREWS 13:5 NKJV

God, it's so easy to break the tenth commandment: Do not covet (see Exodus 20:17). Coveting is a way of life for many in our world. But You say we shouldn't compare ourselves with the "Joneses," nor envy them and what they have. Whatever You've given me is to be enjoyed and received, not held up for inspection. Teach me a deeper gratefulness for Your blessings. In Jesus' name, amen.

....

....

....

....

Evening
TAKING UP MY CROSS

And he said to them all, If any man will come after me, let him deny himself, and take up his cross daily, and follow me.
LUKE 9:23 KJV

You have given me eternal life, Jesus, and no one can take it from me. There's nothing I can do that will make me more or less saved. I will live for You. So many people don't understand this commitment. I want to be identified with You, though, precious Savior. Even if that requires being misunderstood, mocked, or even persecuted, I am willing.

....

....

....

....

....

Morning
WITH JESUS

Father, I will that they also, whom thou hast given me, be with me where I am; that they may behold my glory, which thou hast given me.

JOHN 17:24 KJV

God, as much as I may wish I knew what the future holds, only You know what will happen. Instead of worrying about things that I cannot control, I want to simply follow You into tomorrow and into eternity. The truth is I don't really care where You lead me. . .so long as Jesus is there too.

....

....

....

....

....

....

Evening
SHARING FAITH WITH CHILDREN

And that from a child thou hast known the holy scriptures, which are able to make thee wise unto salvation through faith which is in Christ Jesus.

2 TIMOTHY 3:15 KJV

What a tremendous privilege I have to be able to share Your Word with children. It is an abundance of spiritual wealth right at our fingertips. Through scripture we can know Your great salvation and experience a deeper understanding of Your immense love for us. It is a prize to be treasured.

....

....

....

....

....

Morning
JOY

For ye shall go out with joy, and be led forth with peace:
the mountains and the hills shall break forth before you into
singing, and all the trees of the field shall clap their hands.

ISAIAH 55:12 KJV

Some days, Lord, things are going so well that it feels like all of creation is singing Your praises, and I join with them. Other days, even when creation sings, I don't feel like praising. Thank You, Lord, for the reminder that no matter what today brings, You promise me joy. Help me live out Your joy every day.

....

....

....

....

....

Evening
SLOW DOWN

The thoughts of the [steadily] diligent tend only to plenteousness,
but everyone who is impatient and hasty hastens only to want.

PROVERBS 21:5 AMPC

Lord, I know patience has its own deep benefits. Your halts along the way are intended to help me experience the best You designed for my life. My hurried pace seeks to avoid pain. In doing so, it misses untold blessings You planned for me. Don't let me miss Your best blessings. Slow me down to do Your will, Jesus.

....

....

....

....

Morning

I WILL LIFT UP MINE EYES

Let the rivers clap their hands, let the mountains sing together for joy.

PSALM 98:8 NIV

Lord, I praise You for mountains. I praise You for snowcapped peaks and glacier-grooved summits and the way mountains train my eyes *upward*. Lord, I so often fix my eyes on the pebbles at my feet, on the trivialities that trip me and dog my path. Give me Your eyes, Lord. Give me the long view. Thank You for this trail I am on, the sights along the way, and the vista that awaits at the end. Amen.

....

....

....

....

....

Evening

DELIVERED!

For he will deliver the needy who cry out, the afflicted who have no one to help.

PSALM 72:12 NIV

Lord, not only do You stand beside me when I'm in trouble or pain, You promise to deliver me. You provide all I require. The only reason I could lack anything I truly need, Jesus, is that I've forgotten to ask You. Keep me in devoted connection with You, sharing every need, and I will never be needy or lost in affliction. Thank You, Lord, for caring for all my needs and hurts.

....

....

....

....

....

Morning
LET IT BE

*And Mary said, Behold the handmaid of the
Lord; be it unto me according to thy word.*
LUKE 1:38 KJV

Lord, help me follow Mary's example when she found out that she was
pregnant with the Son of God. Her world was rocked, God! What a scandal!
A good Jewish girl pregnant before she was married? Unthinkable! But
she accepted the news and surrendered her life and her body to Your will.
Help me accept Your Word, no matter what it says to me, and surrender
myself to it.

Evening
HIS AWESOME POWER

*Say to God, "How awesome are your deeds! So great is
your power. . . . All the earth bows down to you; they
sing praise to you, they sing the praises of your name."*
PSALM 66:3–4 NIV

Lord, You parted the Red Sea, and You still the wind and the waves. You
give sight to the blind and hearing to the deaf. You raise people from the
dead. Your power is awesome. Nothing is impossible for You. I bow before
You, singing praises to Your name.

Morning

RIGHT MOTIVES

Ye ask, and receive not, because ye ask amiss,
that ye may consume it upon your lusts.

JAMES 4:3 KJV

God, I admit that sometimes I am guilty of treating You like a vending machine—if I say the right words in the right order, I'll get what I want. If I'm honest, I know that selfishness and greed may slip into a request here or there. Today I ask that You show me when my prayers are corrupted by selfish desires. Give me pure motives, a pure heart, and a clear conscience.

....

....

....

....

Evening

LEARNING FROM THE PAST

Not only so, but we also glory in our sufferings, because we know that
suffering produces perseverance; perseverance, character; and character, hope.

ROMANS 5:3–4 NIV

Lord, I thank You for Your patience as I learn important lessons from my past. I don't want to repeat my mistakes, Lord. Your ways bring healing and life. As I learn to rejoice in the suffering I've experienced, I can see Your hand teaching me perseverance; from perseverance I develop character, and from character I have hope.

....

....

....

....

....

Morning

GOLDEN WORDS NEEDED

A word fitly spoken is like apples of gold in settings of silver.
PROVERBS 25:11 NKJV

Heavenly Father, today I need affirming words. You know that words are important to me as a woman. You also know that I struggle with self-worth. The other people in my world don't always meet my need to be affirmed verbally, and I can't expect them to fulfill every void in my life. So, Lord, let me look to and in Your Word to find the love and encouragement I need. In Jesus' name, amen.

....

....

....

....

Evening

THE COMFORT OF THE SCRIPTURES

For whatsoever things were written aforetime were written for our learning, that we through patience and comfort of the scriptures might have hope.
ROMANS 15:4 KJV

Lord, our twisted, sinful natures have caused sorrow and hate, fear and confusion. In Your great love You've given me a way to have hope and comfort. You gave Your Word so I might learn how to have a restored relationship with You. I don't have to be defeated by the attitudes of this world. Through Your Word You've given me a better way.

....

....

....

....

....

Morning

OVERTAKEN

But My words and My statutes, which I commanded My servants the prophets, did they not overtake and take hold of your fathers? So they repented.

ZECHARIAH 1:6 AMPC

Often, Lord, when I imagine witnessing, I think I have to have every argument planned out in advance. If I don't have perfect answers for potential questions, that's enough to keep me from opening my mouth at all. But Your Word is clear: *we* do not convert the lost. The Gospel is *alive*. It converts. It overtakes. Lord, I trust Your Word and its mighty power to do what I cannot. Amen.

....

....

....

....

Evening

HELPED

And the LORD shall help them and deliver them. . .because they trust in Him.

PSALM 37:40 NKJV

Even in the midst of trouble, You have pulled me through. Others have joined hands to help me, and somehow even the biggest problems have begun to work themselves out. I know it's not because I've done such a great job—You have been smoothing the way for me. Thank You for delivering me from trouble at just the right moment. You are so great, Jesus. I appreciate every scrap of help You've given.

....

....

....

....

....

Morning
CONFIDENCE

And this is the confidence that we have in him, that,
if we ask any thing according to his will, he heareth us.
1 JOHN 5:14 KJV

As I pray, Lord, I rest in the confidence that You are always listening and that You understand the thoughts behind my prayers, even when I cannot. I am never speaking into empty air! Thank You for the confidence I also experience through the power of Your Holy Spirit that lives inside my heart. With You on my side, I can accomplish much for Your kingdom!

....

....

....

....

....

Evening
KEEPING GOD'S WORD

Blessed is he that readeth, and they that hear the words of this prophecy,
and keep those things which are written therein: for the time is at hand.
REVELATION 1:3 KJV

I know that my time on earth is limited and that what I do for You counts more than anything else. You will guide me in reading and living Your Word. All I can do is believe it and set the right example for those who watch. I want Your blessing in my life. Help me passionately study and obey Your commands.

....

....

....

....

Morning
THE TRUTH

*Jesus saith unto him, I am the way, the truth, and the
life: no man cometh unto the Father, but by me.*
JOHN 14:6 KJV

When I pray to You, God, I pray in Your Son's name. He is the Way, He is the Truth, and He will show me the way to You so that I can live the life that You intend for me. Help me avoid distraction by other false paths that may seem more attractive or easier. Make my journey one that invites others to follow me, just as I follow Christ.

....

....

....

....

Evening
TIDINGS OF GREAT JOY

*And the angel said unto them, Fear not: for, behold, I bring
you good tidings of great joy, which shall be to all people.*
LUKE 2:10 KJV

Dear God, when I receive good news, I can't wait to share it with everyone around me. My friends and my family graciously listen as I tell them what I've learned. Yet glorious events in my life can't begin to compare with the joyful tidings proclaimed by the angels the night Your Son was born. It is Your Son who makes my life worth living!

....

....

....

....

....

Morning

A JOYFUL NOISE

Shout joyfully to the LORD, all the earth;
break forth in song, rejoice, and sing praises.
PSALM 98:4 NKJV

Dear God, I thank You for music. For the music of rain on rooftops and wind in bare branches. For the splash of water over stones. For little children shouting a hymn at the top of their lungs. For a Bach organ concerto. Lord, Your creation praises You all the time, with every breath and in every moment. Thank You for letting me join in this eternal song of praise. Hallelujah! Worthy is the Lamb who was slain!

....
....
....
....

Evening

JOY IN GOD'S WORD

These things have I spoken unto you, that my joy might
remain in you, and that your joy might be full.
JOHN 15:11 KJV

You are my guide and instructor, dear God. Your precious Word tells me how to live. It provides the insight I need to be a godly friend and family member. You teach me how to serve You and minister to others. You've given everything I need to live an abundant life, and You did it so my joy would be full. How glad I am to have a personal God!

....
....
....
....
....

Morning
UNITED IN PRAYER

I say unto you, That if two of you shall agree on earth as touching any thing that they shall ask, it shall be done for them of my Father which is in heaven.

MATTHEW 18:19 KJV

Thank You, Lord, for others who share my faith. Thank You for the privilege of praying and worshipping with them, working together to build Your kingdom. Thank You that when we pray together, You hear us, and when we gather together, You are there with us. Help us be the living, breathing, and active body of Christ that we are meant to be.

....

....

....

....

Evening
PEACEABLE WISDOM

But the wisdom that is from above is first pure, then peaceable, gentle, and easy to be intreated, full of mercy and good fruits, without partiality, and without hypocrisy.

JAMES 3:17 KJV

Thank You, Father, that Your wisdom is abundantly good. It brings joy and peace to my heart, but it extends even farther. When I apply Your wisdom to the decisions I make, it affects my family and others around me. It can contribute to their peace too. Please give me this wisdom.

....

....

....

....

....

Morning

DRY MOUTH

We also believe and therefore speak.

2 CORINTHIANS 4:13 NKJV

Lord, You can use anyone to spread the Good News. You can use even me. Thank You that You don't require me to know everything or have every answer. You don't require me to be well traveled or well dressed. You don't require a seminary degree. You don't require me to be anything but saved by the blood of Jesus. The only requirement for evangelism is that I believe and speak. Lord, I believe. Now open my mouth.

....

....

....

....

....

Evening

REFUGE AND STRENGTH

God is our refuge and strength, a very present help in trouble.

PSALM 46:1 NKJV

If I need a safe place to hide from the world for a time, You are there. But I appreciate that You don't let me avoid reality for long. Instead You offer real help—strength to take on every challenge. With You by my side, I will not hide from life. Your help returns me to life the way I should live it—focused on You alone. Help me rely on Your strength in every trial.

....

....

....

....

....

Morning
ABIDING

*If ye abide in me, and my words abide in you, ye shall
ask what ye will, and it shall be done unto you.*

JOHN 15:7 KJV

Father, help me abide in You as I pray. Keep my thoughts focused on You as I wait for Your answers to my prayers. Keep me close, and allow me to abide in You as You ultimately answer my requests. Give me the peace of knowing that You work all things for good.

....

....

....

....

....

Evening
BLESSED WITH FRIENDS

*The sweet smell of perfume and oils is pleasant,
and so is good advice from a friend.*

PROVERBS 27:9 NCV

There are many wonderful things in this life, Lord. A good word, deed, or thought from a friend is even better. There are times when I am so down, and then a friend blesses me and I think of You. It's because of You and the love that You give that makes us want to reach out to others. Thank You for blessing my life with friends.

....

....

....

....

....

Morning
WAVERING HEARTS

Let him ask in faith, nothing wavering. For he that wavereth
is like a wave of the sea driven with the wind and tossed.
JAMES 1:6 KJV

You know how easily my heart wavers, Lord. I'm like a boat out in open water, the world's woes tossing me around like high waves. Take the helm of my boat. Then after I've given over control of the boat, quiet the wind and waves. Help me pray with faith's absolute calm, knowing that You have already ordained the outcome and that You have my best interest at heart.

....

....

....

....

Evening
FOR THOSE IN GRIEF

"Blessed are those who mourn, for they will be comforted."
MATTHEW 5:4 NIV

Lord, my friend has deep pain in her soul. I ask that You would comfort her. Be near, Lord, be near. May she rest in the strong and loving arms of the One who loves her most. Heal her heartache; heal her sorrow. You are One acquainted with grief so You know her pain. Help her know that You can relate and that You care. One day soon, may she find healing and wholeness again.

....

....

....

....

....

Morning
WITH ENDURANCE

*Indeed we count them blessed who endure. You have heard
of the perseverance of Job and seen the end intended by the
Lord—that the Lord is very compassionate and merciful.*

JAMES 5:11 NKJV

Lord, I know my trials are small compared to what some have experienced. That doesn't mean my pain is unimportant to You. No matter what I'm going through, if I hold fast to You, Your compassion and mercy find me out. When I put my faith in Your promises, You always come through. Thank You, Jesus, that You are still in control of my life.

....

....

....

....

Evening
TO A GOD WHO MADE GIRAFFES

Then our mouth was filled with laughter and our tongue with joyful shouting.

PSALM 126:2 NASB

Dear Lord, tonight I laughed until my sides ached, and it was *good*. Now I feel cleansed, content, and emptied of distress. Thank You for being a God whose miracles bring laughter: Sarah with the news of her improbable baby, Lazarus raised to life, and the disciples with their ridiculous catch of fish. I can imagine You standing there, Lord, and laughing until the tears came with the people You love. You long to astonish us with joy. Amen.

....

....

....

....

....

Morning
ANYTHING!

For verily I say unto you, That whosoever shall say unto this mountain, Be thou removed, and be thou cast into the sea; and shall not doubt in his heart, but shall believe that those things which he saith shall come to pass; he shall have whatsoever he saith.

MARK 11:23 KJV

I don't want to throw any mountains into the ocean, God—and it's hard for me to believe that Jesus really meant what He said here. Show me the truth of His words. Teach me to pray according to Your will.

....

....

....

....

Evening
JESUS, OUR CONFIDENCE

In [Jesus] and through faith in him we may approach God with freedom and confidence.

EPHESIANS 3:12 NIV

Thank You, Jesus, for Your love. As Your love brings me confidently into the presence of the Father, remind me that trusting in anything or anyone other than You lands me in a lifestyle of overconfidence in myself. If that was all I had today, pain and loneliness would flood my soul. I need Your love and guidance for my life. During this trial, strengthen my faith and help me follow confidently in Your way.

....

....

....

....

....

Morning
POWER

The effectual fervent prayer of a righteous man availeth much.
JAMES 5:16 KJV

Sometimes I say, "The only thing I can do now is pray." I mean that I've done everything I could think to do, and now as a last resort, I'll fall back on prayer. Forgive me, Father, for trusting in things that are not from You and for setting my mind on worldly things. Remind me that prayer is never the last resort and that You are faithful in hearing it. Teach me to see the power that prayer can unleash in the world.

....

....

....

....

....

Evening
GOD'S REDEMPTION

*Israel, put your hope in the LORD, for with the LORD
is unfailing love and with him is full redemption.*
PSALM 130:7 NIV

Thank You, Jesus, for Your unfailing love. Your saving work didn't touch me for only a moment; it reclaimed every second of my life. Whatever trials I pass through, You remain beside me, working out Your total redemption. Hope need not wait for eternity; it's evident in my daily experiences. Help me faithfully trust in You, Lord.

....

....

....

....

Morning
ENCOURAGED!

*Be of good courage, and He shall strengthen
your heart, all you who hope in the LORD.*
PSALM 31:24 NKJV

Where can I find strength to go on in trials? Only in You, Lord. When my heart falters, I lift my face to You and receive the energy to go on. Your Spirit leads me in the right direction. No human or physical solution has Your eternal strength. Everything humanity comes up with falls short of Your heart-empowering ability, Lord. Thank You for lifting me up. I need Your courage filling my life.

....

....

....

....

Evening
WELL BEGUN IS HALF DONE

Now faith is the substance of things hoped for, the evidence of things not seen.
HEBREWS 11:1 NKJV

Dear God, there is something You've asked me to do that I've been putting off. You keep reminding and prodding me to obey. Tonight, as I was walking and pondering this in the darkness between streetlights, I was filled with a cheerful certainty that by the next day, I will have begun. This wasn't wishful thinking, was it, Lord? It was *faith*. Thank You for believing in what is not yet visible in me and allowing me to do the same. Amen.

....

....

....

....

....

Morning

LESSONS IN TRUST

I have put my trust in the Lord God, that I may declare all Your works.
PSALM 73:28 NKJV

Heavenly Father, teach me to trust. In spite of the fact that I know Your character and Your track record, I find it so difficult to relinquish to You the important areas of life. I say that I will, and I do put forth effort to rely on You, but I still find it hard to let You handle everything. So take my hand, Lord, and teach me to trust. In Christ's name, amen.

....

....

....

....

....

Evening

NO MORE SORROW

And ye now therefore have sorrow: but I will see you again, and your heart shall rejoice, and your joy no man taketh from you.
JOHN 16:22 KJV

Jesus, Your disciples were dismayed. You told them You were going away but that You would see them again. Those men had walked and talked with You. You were their leader, their friend. How lost they must have felt at Your crucifixion! But three days later. . . Wow! Lord, You turn mourning into rejoicing. Help me trust in this. Thank You, Jesus.

....

....

....

....

....

Morning

IN ALL MY WAYS

In all thy ways acknowledge him, and he shall direct thy paths.
PROVERBS 3:6 KJV

God, I claim Your presence in each aspect of my life. Thank You for Your steadfast love and abounding grace. I honor You alone with my successes and acknowledge Your guiding hand on my life. Help me set my eyes only on You. Teach me to trust You with all my heart and not lean on my own wisdom or understanding. May my heart always seek to bring glory to Your name, and may my prayers always reflect this reality.

....

....

....

....

....

Evening

TRUTH IN SCRIPTURE

Thou hast made known to me the ways of life;
thou shalt make me full of joy with thy countenance.
ACTS 2:28 KJV

Thank You, God, that in Your holy scriptures I find the ways of life. I find wise counsel in the pages of my Bible. You reveal the truth to me, Lord, and there is no greater blessing than to know the truth. I am free to live a life that brings You glory and honor. May others see the joy I have found in You!

....

....

....

....

....

Morning
WILLING MIND

Acknowledge the God of your father, and serve him with
wholehearted devotion and with a willing mind, for the
LORD searches every heart and understands every desire and
every thought. If you seek him, he will be found by you.

1 CHRONICLES 28:9 NIV

Make my mind willing, Lord. Help me trust that Your plans for me are better than my own. Place Your desires in my heart, that I may be able to walk fully in Your will for my life. Help me agree with Your ways for my life. I seek You who understands me completely.

....

....

....

....

Evening
GLORIFYING GOD IN MY WORK

And whatsoever ye do, do it heartily, as to the Lord, and
not unto men; knowing that of the Lord ye shall receive the
reward of the inheritance: for ye serve the Lord Christ.

COLOSSIANS 3:23–24 KJV

God, may my attitude glorify You. May I think twice before I grumble, Father, about the tasks set before me this day. I will choose to work as unto my Father, and may my countenance reflect Your love to those around me.

....

....

....

....

....

Morning
THE GIVER

You open your hand and satisfy the desires of every living thing.
PSALM 145:16 NIV

Lord, You have been a faithful provider of the things You know I need. Thank You, Lord, for providing for me through generosity and hard work. It's humbling to realize that I've never been completely self-sufficient at any point in my life, yet there is a lesson in that too. We are paupers by nature: *all* is from You. I praise my open-handed God! Amen.

....

....

....

....

....

Evening
TRUST IN GOD

*In peace I will both lie down and sleep, for You, Lord,
alone make me dwell in safety and confident trust.*
PSALM 4:8 AMPC

Because I can rest assured You are caring for me, I sleep peacefully, Lord. I need not keep myself awake at night, worrying about my life, relationships, or future troubles. I can turn to You in prayer and receive comfort. You keep me from harm. Thank You, Lord, for giving me Your rest and peace despite the troubles I have faced. When I'm connected to You, Jesus, I have nothing to fear!

....

....

....

....

Morning
PERFECT HEART

*Let your heart therefore be perfect with the LORD our God, to walk
in his statutes, and to keep his commandments, as at this day.*
1 KINGS 8:61 KJV

You know I can never achieve perfection on my own, Lord. I surrender my
heart to You absolutely. Keep my heart and mind from wandering, and allow
me to remain true only to You. I thank You for Your never-ending grace
that sustains my life and that You never leave me or forsake me. Through
my prayer, I commit myself totally to You and Your law for my life.

....

....

....

....

Evening
WHERE IS PEACE FOUND?

*For the kingdom of God is not a matter of eating and drinking, but of
righteousness, peace and joy in the Holy Spirit, because anyone who serves
Christ in this way is pleasing to God and receives human approval.*
ROMANS 14:17–18 NIV

Lord, everyone is looking for peace. Your Word tells us it's not what we
eat or drink that provides lasting satisfaction. May I find peace and joy in
Your Holy Spirit, Lord. Knowing You, loving You, and experiencing You
is true peace. Thank You, Lord.

....

....

....

....

....

Morning
DIVINE GUIDANCE

*If any of you lacks wisdom, you should ask God, who gives generously
to all without finding fault, and it will be given to you.*
JAMES 1:5 NIV

Dear Lord, it's so hard sometimes to know what Your will is. How can I know exactly what You want me to do? I ask today that You would give me wisdom; send me guidance as I seek Your will. Through a person, a thought, a scripture, let me sense Your leading for this situation. I want my life to honor Your plan for me. In Christ's name, amen.

....

....

....

....

Evening
A GIVING HEART

*Remember the words of the Lord Jesus, how he said,
It is more blessed to give than to receive.*
ACTS 20:35 KJV

Father, sometimes I don't feel like serving. People keep asking me to help with things at church, and there is always a collection being taken up. Can't I just focus on me? I have my own needs! But oh, the peace I feel when I lay my head on my pillow at night knowing I have loved with action, with sacrifice. Make me a giver.

....

....

....

....

....

Morning
CELEBRATION

They celebrate your abundant goodness and joyfully sing of your righteousness.
PSALM 145:7 NIV

Dear Father, so many people who don't know You see You as a heavenly killjoy: stopping them from doing fun things that would bring them enjoyment. We know You better! Thank You for not delighting in denial: You delight in saying yes to Your people. More importantly, You delight in *us* and what is for our ultimate good, not just what is fun for a moment. And You are planning the ultimate party—one that will last forever. I can't wait to join the celebration! Amen.

Evening
JOYFUL IN HOPE

Happy is he that hath the God of Jacob for his help, whose hope is in the LORD his God.
PSALM 146:5 KJV

God, the longer I live, the more I realize that joy and hope go hand in hand. I have joy because my hope is in You. Thank You, Lord, that as Your daughter, I do not go out to face the day in hopelessness. No matter what happens, I can find joy because my hope is not in this world or in my circumstances. My hope is in the Lord!

Morning
WILLING

I know also, my God, that thou triest the heart, and hast pleasure in uprightness. As for me, in the uprightness of mine heart I have willingly offered all these things.

1 CHRONICLES 29:17 KJV

God, I give You everything I have to offer, willingly and gladly. I know that everything I have You have provided and have entrusted to me. Give me a whole heart to follow after You and keep Your commandments. Keep forever in my heart Your purposes and thoughts. Show me anything I am holding back. I want You to have it all.

....

....

....

....

Evening
TO BE MORE CONSIDERATE

You know this, my beloved brothers and sisters. Now everyone must be quick to hear, slow to speak, and slow to anger.

JAMES 1:19 NASB

I could be more considerate. I admit it—I'm usually thinking of myself instead of someone else. Help me be more considerate of others. Help me listen when someone is speaking to me. Show me what You want me to say when someone gives me the opportunity to speak to them.

....

....

....

....

....

Morning

DEEP SURRENDER

But now, O LORD, You are our Father; we are the clay,
and You our potter; and all we are the work of Your hand.

ISAIAH 64:8 NKJV

Lord, I need to surrender to You. You've shown me an area of my life that I've been trying to rule. I know You need the keys to every room in my heart, and so here I am, bringing this one to You. *Surrender* means I give You permission to change, clean out, and add things. Surrender isn't easy, but it's the way to true joy. Thank You for showing me that. Amen.

....

....

....

....

....

Evening

TINY STEPS

"And if anyone gives even a cup of cold water to one of these little ones who is
my disciple, truly I tell you, that person will certainly not lose their reward."

MATTHEW 10:42 NIV

Jesus, You've promised that even the smallest act done out of love for You reaps an eternal reward. Don't let my weakness deter me from doing the small, kind deed that springs from faith. Tiny steps now may lead to large ones later. Help me reach out to others who need Your love now.

....

....

....

....

....

Morning

TRUTHFUL HEART

*Lord, who shall abide in thy tabernacle? who shall dwell
in thy holy hill? He that walketh uprightly, and worketh
righteousness, and speaketh the truth in his heart.*

PSALM 15:1–2 KJV

Lord, sometimes I lie to myself. Sometimes I try to lie to You. But You
know me. You know my thoughts before I think them. Reveal to me Your
truth so that my prayers may be true, righteous, and upright. Show me
how to live a blameless life.

....

....

....

....

....

Evening

SERVE ONE ANOTHER

*By love serve one another. For all the law is fulfilled in one word,
even in this; Thou shalt love thy neighbour as thyself.*

GALATIANS 5:13–14 KJV

God, sometimes I forget that it's not all about me! Service is what this life is
all about. Father, give me opportunities to show love to others today. Make
every moment a "God moment." Help me be aware of the many needs around
me. Create in me a heart that loves others and puts them ahead of myself.

....

....

....

....

....

Morning
HIS WORK

*For the eyes of the Lord are on the righteous
and his ears are attentive to their prayer.*

1 PETER 3:12 NIV

God, I am amazed that You never tire of listening to me. You hear the same fears, complaints, problems, and confusions—year after year. Yet even I see progress, and I praise You. I am not who I was, and I know it's all because of You. Thank You for how You continue to work in me: so faithfully, patiently, lovingly. You are the Potter; I am the grateful clay in Your hands. Amen.

....

....

....

....

....

Evening
USE ME, LORD

*For whosoever will save his life shall lose it; but whosoever shall
lose his life for my sake and the gospel's, the same shall save it.*

MARK 8:35 KJV

Savior, You laid down Your life for me. It was death by crucifixion, which was reserved for the worst of criminals. You had done nothing wrong. You came into the world to save us! You gave Your very life for us. Jesus, take my life. Use me for Your kingdom's work.

....

....

....

....

....

Morning
ONE MIND

*That ye may with one mind and one mouth glorify
God, even the Father of our Lord Jesus Christ.*
ROMANS 15:6 KJV

Unite me in prayer with others, Father God. Let no division come between us as we talk with You. Give me patience in dealing with difficult people; remind me that patience will build up Your church. Forgive me for any gossip or malicious words I've spoken against my brothers and sisters, and give me a heart that longs for their good. Bring to my mind ways I can show love that will bring more glory to You.

....

....

....

....

Evening
EVERY GOOD GIFT

*And thou shalt rejoice in every good thing which the LORD
thy God hath given unto thee, and unto thine house, thou,
and the Levite, and the stranger that is among you.*
DEUTERONOMY 26:11 KJV

Father, thank You for the blessings You have poured out on my family. Often I dwell on what we do not have. Please remind me to be ever grateful. The comforts we enjoy each day are easily taken for granted. Thank You for Your provision. Help me have a thankful heart so that my family might be more thankful also.

....

....

....

....

Morning
BELIEVING

Be not faithless, but believing.
JOHN 20:27 KJV

I believe in You, Jesus. I believe in Your power and wisdom and love. I believe that Your atoning work on the cross has washed me of all my unrighteousness and that through it, I stand in perfect righteousness before God. Take my life—all my words and deeds—and use them for Your glory. Teach me to trust You, not requiring proof as Thomas did but believing You at Your Word alone. Thank You that Your Word is truth and brings life to me and to those around me.

....

....

....

....

Evening
A SAFE PLACE

My people will live in peaceful dwelling places,
in secure homes, in undisturbed places of rest.
ISAIAH 32:18 NIV

Lord, I ask that You would be our strong defense and protect our home. May this be a place of safety, comfort, and peace. Guard us from outside forces, and protect us from harmful attacks from within. I pray that the Holy Spirit would put a hedge of protection around our home and family. Lord, we look to You as our refuge, our strength and security.

....

....

....

....

....

Morning

ENDURANCE REQUIRED

Let us run with endurance the race that is set before us.

HEBREWS 12:1 NKJV

I'm finding, Lord, that the Christian life is one that requires endurance. It isn't enough to start well. So let me patiently and steadily move down the road to Christlikeness. I know difficulties will come; I've faced some already. It reminds me of the words of the second verse of "Amazing Grace": "Through many dangers, toils, and snares, I have already come. 'Tis grace that brought me safe thus far, and grace will lead me home." In Your name, amen.

....

....

....

....

....

Evening

GOD'S GRASP

"And this is the will of him who sent me, that I shall lose none of all those he has given me, but raise them up at the last day."

JOHN 6:39 NIV

Lord, I live in confidence that even serious loss can never steal my most important treasure. Temporal things are only given to me to use for a while. But any heart You hold, You keep forever, firm in Your hand. In eternity, I will be lifted into an infinity of praise and worship. Thank You, Lord, for holding me tightly in love.

....

....

....

....

Morning
THE GRAND TIME LINE

He has made everything beautiful in its time. He has also
set eternity in the human heart; yet no one can fathom
what God has done from beginning to end.
ECCLESIASTES 3:11 NIV

Lord, thank You for the grand story of history, which is really *Your* story.
You had the end in mind from the beginning. I know I can trust that You
are leading us to a good place. I praise You for the amazing grace that has
allowed my story to be a small part of the story You are telling. Amen.

....

....

....

....

Evening
THE PEACE THAT BRINGS LIFE

A heart at peace gives life to the body, but envy rots the bones.
PROVERBS 14:30 NIV

Lord, I thank You for the peace that restores me mentally, emotionally,
and physically. It is the peace that brings wholeness. When my heart is
restless, my health suffers. But when I am at peace, You restore my entire
body. I can breathe easier, I can relax, and I can smile again because I know
everything's going to be all right. You are in control. I thank You that Your
peace brings life.

....

....

....

....

....

Morning

JOIN THE MORNING

JOY IN THE MORNING

"For the joy of the Lord is your strength."
NEHEMIAH 8:10 NIV

Lord, some mornings I wake up ready to go! I feel rested and energetic. Other mornings, I wonder how I will make it through the day. Remind me that as Your child, I have a power source that is always available to me. I may not always feel joyful, but the joy of the Lord is my strength. As I spend time in Your Word, renew my strength. In Jesus' name, amen.

....

....

....

....

....

Evening

THE VALUE OF FELLOWSHIP

Two are better than one; because they have a good reward for their labour. For if they fall, the one will lift up his fellow.
ECCLESIASTES 4:9–10 KJV

Heavenly Father, I pray that You help me avoid isolating myself. I benefit from spending time with my Christian friends. You tell us in Your Word it is not good to be alone. We need one another as we walk through this life with all of its ups and downs. When I am tempted to distance myself from others, guide me back into Christian fellowship.

....

....

....

....

....

Morning
TRUE JOY

*These things have I spoken unto you, that my joy might
remain in you, and that your joy might be full.*

JOHN 15:11 KJV

Thank You, Father, for Your Word, which teaches me how to experience true
joy. This world sends me a lot of messages through the media and through
those who do not know You. I have tried some of the things that are sup-
posed to bring joy, but they always leave me empty in the end. Thank You
for the truth. Help me abide in You, that I might be overflowing with joy.
Amen.

....

....

....

....

Evening
SHIELD OF FAITH

*Above all, taking the shield of faith, wherewith ye shall
be able to quench all the fiery darts of the wicked.*

EPHESIANS 6:16 KJV

God, guard my heart and mind with the shield of faith. I will call on the
name of Jesus when Satan tempts me. I will fight against his schemes to
ruin me. My weapon is my knowledge of Your Word, promises memorized
and cherished. My defense is my faith in Jesus Christ, my Savior. On this
faith I will stand. Increase my faith, and protect me from the evil one.

....

....

....

....

....

Morning

HELP WITH PRIORITIES

For where your treasure is, there your heart will be also.
MATTHEW 6:21 NIV

Dear God, I need help with my priorities. It is so easy for them to get out of whack. Show me the things I've let creep to the top that don't belong there. Point out to me those areas where I need to put more emphasis and commitment. Lord, let me remember that people are worth more than possessions and pursuits. Let my unseen checklist of priorities reflect that. Amen.

....

....

....

....

....

Evening

FRIENDS HELP EACH OTHER

If either of them falls down, one can help the other up.
But pity anyone who falls and has no one to help them up.
ECCLESIASTES 4:10 NIV

Lord, sometimes it's easier to give than to receive. I want to be a giver, to take the time to care and help my friends when they need it. And help me learn to receive too—so that I'm not too proud to receive generosity from a friend. Give and take, Lord. . .we really do need each other.

....

....

....

....

....

....

Morning

DON'T WORRY!

Don't worry about anything, but pray about everything.
PHILIPPIANS 4:6 CEV

Dear Lord, Your Word tells me it is wrong to worry. Some people say women are just born worriers. I guess there's some truth to that, maybe because we're so invested in relationships, and most of our worrying is about those we love and care for. Still, You know worry isn't good for us, and it doesn't accomplish anything. So, today, help me avoid worry and turn all my concerns over to You.

....

....

....

....

Evening

FIGHTING DISCOURAGEMENT

"Then you will have success if you are careful to observe the decrees and laws that the LORD gave Moses for Israel. Be strong and courageous. Do not be afraid or discouraged."
1 CHRONICLES 22:13 NIV

Discouragement and sorrow make me feel so empty inside, but You remind me that You will give me strength. I have no reason to dread. When I feel weak, Your power can fill me, Jesus. Neither fear nor discouragement needs to control my heart. You'll win the fight against fear and depression, if I only trust in You.

....

....

....

....

....

Morning
EXTRAS

And my God will meet all your needs according
to the riches of his glory in Christ Jesus.
PHILIPPIANS 4:19 NIV

Dear God, I am so thankful that You have provided for me. Sometimes that blessing even goes above and beyond my needs. I now ask for wisdom in handling these gifts. My desire is to glorify You and to make sure that I'm not controlled by money. Please help me use it in a way that honors You. Amen.

....

....

....

....

Evening
THE PATIENCE CHALLENGE

Love is patient, love is kind.
1 CORINTHIANS 13:4 NIV

My love isn't always patient, Lord. When others challenge my ability to love, patience becomes even more difficult. You are always patient, kind, and caring. Even when I haven't deserved it, You've offered me second chances. I want to reflect Your love, poured out so generously on me. Though I may not feel I do it well now, I want to become patient. Help me grow in Your patient love, beginning today.

....

....

....

....

....

Morning
A PROPER OUTLOOK

He that loveth silver shall not be satisfied with silver; nor he
that loveth abundance with increase: this is also vanity.

ECCLESIASTES 5:10 KJV

So often, Lord, I see relationships crumbling, and much of the time a money issue is what starts the process. Some people are careless or dishonest in their spending; others just want too much. As a result there is a lot of bitterness and hatred. Please help me have a proper outlook when money is involved.

....

....

....

....

....

Evening
JOYFUL REGARDLESS OF CIRCUMSTANCES

Rejoice evermore. Pray without ceasing. In every thing give thanks:
for this is the will of God in Christ Jesus concerning you.

1 THESSALONIANS 5:16–18 KJV

Lord, there are days when I can't help but rejoice in what You are doing. But many times the daily grind is just rather humdrum. There is nothing to rejoice about, much less give thanks for! Or is there? Help me, Father, to be joyful and thankful every day. Each day is a gift from You. Remind me of this truth today, and give me a joyful, thankful heart.

....

....

....

....

....

Morning

DON'T LET THE LITTLE ONES PERISH

"In the same way your Father in heaven is not willing
that any of these little ones should perish."

MATTHEW 18:14 NIV

Lord, I'm so glad You often used children in Your teachings and emphasized the importance of bringing them to You. Otherwise we might fail to share Your salvation with them. I remember how excited I was as a small child when I gave my life to You. When my children recognized Your salvation was for them, my heart sang. What a precious gift.

....

....

....

....

....

Evening

A MEEK AND QUIET SPIRIT

Let it be the hidden man of the heart, in that which is not corruptible, even the
ornament of a meek and quiet spirit, which is in the sight of God of great price.

1 PETER 3:4 KJV

God, in Your economy a meek and quiet spirit is worth more than gold. It is not corruptible. It is eternal. Give me such a spirit. Make me a better listener. Set a guard over my tongue. Teach me to walk humbly with You, Father, and to serve people in Your name. Amen.

....

....

....

....

....

Morning

SAVED THROUGH CHRIST ALONE

"Salvation is found in no one else, for there is no other name
under heaven given to mankind by which we must be saved."

ACTS 4:12 NIV

Lord Jesus, the gift of salvation was a great sacrifice for You, but now it is readily available to us. Yet so many people try to save themselves. Some call on You for their salvation but trust in themselves to work out the details. Others live only for the moment and refuse to acknowledge their need. I'm so glad You saved me, Lord. Thank You for eternal life!

....

....

....

....

Evening

THE GIFT OF SALVATION

For the grace of God has appeared that offers salvation to all people.

TITUS 2:11 NIV

Dear Father, thank You for the gift of salvation, for sending Your only Son to be a sacrifice for all people. I am in awe of Your mercy extended to me. It is incredible to think that I am a daughter of God. Thank You, Holy Spirit, for drawing me to this greatest of gifts. My life is forever changed. In Christ's name, amen.

....

....

....

....

....

....

Morning
SAVED FOR CHRIST'S PURPOSE

[God] hath saved us, and called us with an holy calling, not
according to our works, but according to his own purpose and
grace, which was given us in Christ Jesus before the world began.
2 TIMOTHY 1:9 KJV

Oh great God, before You spoke this world into existence, You had me
in mind. You had a plan. You gave Your Son to pay the price for my sin. I
cannot fathom the depth of Your love. I can't imagine sacrificing a child,
but You did. How passionate Your love is!

....

....

....

....

Evening
MIGHTY THINGS

"Call to Me, and I will answer you, and show you
great and mighty things, which you do not know."
JEREMIAH 33:3 NKJV

Forgive me, Lord, for my unwillingness to pray. Life often interferes with
my prayer plans, and I end up shortchanging You. Make me faithful to my
meetings with You in prayer and meditation. Give me a desire for Your
Word that spurs me to spend time with You. Thank You, Jesus, for wanting
to share Your mighty things with me. I'm calling on You now so You can
show me each one.

....

....

....

....

....

Morning

PROVISION AND RESOURCES

*The next day we landed at Sidon; and Julius, in kindness to Paul,
allowed him to go to his friends so they might provide for his needs.*

ACTS 27:3 NIV

Lord, Your resources are unlimited. You delight in giving Your children
good gifts and meeting their needs. I boldly and humbly ask that You would
provide for the needs of my ministry. Bring our ministry to the minds of
people who are willing to give out of their God-given resources. May they
give of their time, money, talents, or other resources to bless these efforts
to further Your kingdom.

....

....

....

....

Evening

WISE STEWARDSHIP

*The LORD is my strength and my shield; my heart trusts in him, and
he helps me. My heart leaps for joy, and with my song I praise him.*

PSALM 28:7 NIV

Lord, help me be a wise steward of my resources, of all that You have
provided. Help my family take care of our things, to keep them clean and
in good repair. May we use our money wisely, share freely of Your blessings,
and spend our time toward positive ends that bring glory to Your name.

....

....

....

....

....

Morning

A HEART TO SERVE

The LORD is gracious and compassionate, slow to anger and rich in love.
PSALM 145:8 NIV

Lord, I pray for a spirit of compassion. Help me care about the needs of others and have genuine love for the ones I serve. Pour into me Your caring, kind spirit, so I can be a blessing and minister out of a full heart. Fill me to overflowing so my ministry will be effective, growing, and blessed. May I walk in Your graciousness with a heart to serve.

....

....

....

....

....

Evening

A FATHER

As a father has compassion on his children,
so the LORD has compassion on those who fear him.
PSALM 103:13 NIV

God, help me remember that You're my Father. A heavenly Father—One who has unlimited resources and power, and One who has infinitely more love than any earthly father. Lord, fill my heart with the truth that You love me perfectly and have only the best in mind for me. You want to embrace me, bless me, and give me heaven as my inheritance. What a wonderful Father You are!

....

....

....

....

Morning

REIGNING PEACE

*"These things I have spoken to you, that in Me you may
have peace. In the world you will have tribulation;
but be of good cheer, I have overcome the world."*

JOHN 16:33 NKJV

Dear God, I pray for peace around the world. Some say it's impossible—
but with You all things are possible. And while peace may not yet reign
throughout the earth, with You in my heart peace reigns within, for You
have overcome the world! May all people feel Your peace within!

....

....

....

Evening

NEVER GIVE UP

*Wherefore, my beloved, as ye have always obeyed, not as in my
presence only, but now much more in my absence, work out your
own salvation with fear and trembling. For it is God which
worketh in you both to will and to do of his good pleasure.*

PHILIPPIANS 2:12–13 KJV

Lord, I don't want to be a quitter; but I keep messing up. You said that with
You all things are possible, and I need to be reminded of that daily. Don't
let me give up. Help me remember that You aren't finished with me yet.

....

....

....

....

....

Morning
FIND SUCCESS

Commit to the LORD whatever you do, and he will establish your plans.
PROVERBS 16:3 NIV

Lord, I ask for success and favor for all I do today. Bless my work, please. May the time and effort I put into it bear abundant fruit. I commit my plans to You, Lord, and surrender my will for Yours. In all I seek to accomplish, in all I hope to become as a woman of God, may my plans succeed. I pray for victory and triumph as You reveal to me what true success should look like in my life.

....

....

....

....

....

Evening
REACHED GOALS

*For wisdom is better than rubies; and all the things
that may be desired are not to be compared to it.*
PROVERBS 8:11 KJV

Sometimes I get discouraged, Jesus. I feel like I've reached all the goals I've set for myself and that there's nothing for me to achieve that would bring any excitement. Please give me a new outlook. Give me wisdom as I set new goals, and help me give You the glory when I succeed. Amen.

....

....

....

....

....

Morning

WHO'S THE BOSS?

In God I trust and am not afraid. What can man do to me? I am under vows to you, my God; I will present my thank offerings to you.

PSALM 56:11–12 NIV

Lord, I pray for a right mindset with my boss. Help me submit to her authority and work with honesty and integrity. Yet may I have the firm conviction that You are my highest authority. My ultimate trust is in You, Lord, not in any man or woman. As I report to You each day for guidance, help me serve You well.

....

....

....

....

....

Evening

EFFECTIVE PRAYER

The effective, fervent prayer of a righteous man avails much.

JAMES 5:16 NKJV

A good prayer is worth much in Your eyes, Lord. In times of trouble, I've known the blessing of some fervent prayers on my behalf. When my heart agonized, I suddenly felt Your peace and knew someone lifted me up to You. Thank You for those faithful believers who remembered my need. I also want to be an effective, fervent prayer so I can bless others. Help me pass on the blessing, Jesus. So many people need it today.

....

....

....

....

Morning

BE CONTENT

*I am not saying this because I am in need, for I have
learned to be content whatever the circumstances.*

PHILIPPIANS 4:11 NIV

Lord, I often dream of a better future. Sometimes, though, my thoughts
are locked in the past, stuck in disappointment and regret. Please help me
be content with today, to live in this moment, no matter what my current
circumstances are. In every situation, may I look to You for peace. Still the
storms in my heart, so whether I am at rest or in motion, I can find Your
serenity and strength.

....

....

....

....

Evening

MEEKNESS

*With all lowliness and meekness, with longsuffering,
forbearing one another in love.*

EPHESIANS 4:2 KJV

Heavenly Father, I want to develop the characteristic of meekness, a kind of
quiet strength. It takes guts to be silent when you want to speak. Meekness
is not a goal for the weak of heart. It is, rather, for those who would be in
the forefront of spiritual growth. Like Moses, the meekest man on earth
(see Numbers 12:3), we can reap the rewards of quiet strength in our lives.

....

....

....

....

....

Morning
BALANCING WORK AND LIFE

Am I now trying to win the approval of human beings, or of God? Or am I trying to please people? If I were still trying to please people, I would not be a servant of Christ.

GALATIANS 1:10 NIV

Lord, every day is a juggling act. I rarely have time just to be with You. Teach me to center on You, Lord, and keep my focus. You've never asked me to please everyone. You are the One I seek to please. Be the hub of my heart, the steady center that moves the wheel of my life forward.

....

....

....

....

Evening
LEGACY

Prophecy and speaking in unknown languages and special knowledge will become useless. But love will last forever!

1 CORINTHIANS 13:8 NLT

Dear God, what kind of legacy am I leaving? I want to be remembered as more than a woman who went to church. I want to be remembered for the way I invested myself in the lives of others. After all, love is the only lasting thing on this earth, something that will remain after I am gone. Lord, let my legacy be wrapped up in serving others in love.

....

....

....

....

....

Morning
REDUCING STRESS

Do not be anxious about anything, but in every situation, by prayer and petition, with thanksgiving, present your requests to God.

Philippians 4:6 NIV

Lord, deadlines and details swirl around me like a swarm of bees. I feel heavy pressure with my heavy workload. Help me do what needs to be done each day, so I can stop worrying and rest well at night. I give You my anxiety and stress. As Your peace covers me, may it guard my heart and mind in Christ Jesus. I rest in the comfort of Your love.

....

....

....

....

Evening
DISPLACED FEAR

"Be strong and of good courage, do not fear nor be afraid of them; for the LORD your God, He is the One who goes with you. He will not leave you nor forsake you."

Deuteronomy 31:6 NKJV

It would be so easy to give up, Lord, but You remind me I am not walking down this frightening path alone. I need not worry. Painful emotions flee before Your touch. Thank You for standing by me, no matter what I face. When I put all my fears in Your hands, I know I am safe. My strength lies in You alone.

....

....

....

....

....

Morning

JOYFUL SERVANT

*"Well done, my good and faithful servant. You have been
faithful in handling this small amount, so now I will give
you many more responsibilities. Let's celebrate together!"*

MATTHEW 25:23 NLT

I want to be a good and faithful servant, but I feel like the world is bringing
me down. Help me be faithful in what You have given me. I want to feel
and share the joy that working for You brings. Help me renew my mind
this morning. Touch me with Your compassion and grace. Fill me with
Your Spirit, Your joy, Your love.

....

....

....

....

Evening

CONSULTING CHRIST

*Trust in the LORD with all thine heart;
and lean not unto thine own understanding.*

PROVERBS 3:5 KJV

Lord, often in my daily planning I forget to consult You. Then I wonder
why things don't work out the way I think they should. Forgive my arrogant
attitude. I know that only as You guide me through the day will I find joy in
accomplishments. Show me how to align my goals with Your will. Amen.

....

....

....

....

....

Morning

BLESSINGS FROM THE WORK OF YOUR HANDS

*The LORD your God will bless you in all your harvest and in
all the work of your hands, and your joy will be complete.*
DEUTERONOMY 16:15 NIV

Lord, I ask that You would bless the work of my hands. As I sit at a computer, fold laundry, or teach a class, may my work be meaningful and bear good fruit. I pray for a spirit of joy as I go about my business. I pray for a cheerful countenance and a willing servant's heart. I dedicate my work life to You, Lord, for Your good purposes and blessings.

....

....

....

....

Evening

PRAYER POWER

The LORD is far from the wicked, but He hears the prayer of the righteous.
PROVERBS 15:29 NKJV

Speaking to You in prayer gives power to my life. When I turn to You in trouble, I tap into Your strength. Though I may not get an expected answer, You often give me even more than I ask. Better responses seem to be Your specialty, Lord. So draw me close to You. When I seek the desires of Your heart, You are always listening.

....

....

....

....

....

Morning

THE RIGHT ATTITUDE

Do everything without complaining and arguing.
PHILIPPIANS 2:14 NLT

I'm getting tired of my job, Lord. It seems like the same thing day in and day out. I know I should be grateful for the work I have been given, but I can't seem to get past this wall of negativity. Give me the right mindset, Lord, before I even go into work. And then help me remember that I am working for You. Give me the mind and servant attitude of Christ this morning, and help me maintain it throughout this day.

....

....

....

....

....

Evening

SENSORY JOYS

For in him we live, and move, and have our being.
ACTS 17:28 KJV

Dear God, thank You for the five senses—sight, sound, touch, smell, and taste. You could have designed a virtual world, but instead You created one that can be experienced. Today I want to revel in the fact that I'm alive. I want to delight in the tactile joys I often take for granted. I'm grateful for each one. Amen.

....

....

....

....

....

Morning

RESPONDING WELL TO CRITICISM

Fools show their annoyance at once, but the prudent overlook an insult.
PROVERBS 12:16 NIV

Lord, I don't like being criticized. I ask for a calm spirit when others make cutting remarks. Please give me insight to know if what is said is true—and if I need to make changes in my life. If not, Lord, I ask You to heal my heart from these verbal barbs. Please give me patience and discernment to keep my cool and not lash out in retaliation. Please bring our relationship through this criticism.

....

....

....

....

....

Evening

GOSSIP

Let all. . .evil speaking be put away from you, with all malice.
EPHESIANS 4:31 NKJV

Lord, I got caught in gossip today. Before long, the conversation had dug itself a little too deep into someone else's life. I tried to stop listening but didn't try hard enough. Please forgive me, Father. Give me the courage to make the right decision next time; help me refuse to listen to negative stories about someone who is not there to defend herself. In Jesus' name, amen.

....

....

....

....

....

Morning
A NEW MIND

Let God transform you into a new person by changing the
way you think. Then you will learn to know God's will
for you, which is good and pleasing and perfect.
ROMANS 12:2 NLT

I have the wrong mindset today, Lord. Instead of looking to Your leading, I am focused on the worldly aspects of life. That's not where You want my thoughts to be. Give me the mind of Christ. Make my needs simple. Change my life, my thoughts, and my desires. I want to live a life that is good, perfect, and pleasing to You.

....

....

....

....

....

Evening
PRAISE FOR FORGIVENESS AND HEALING

Let all that I am praise the LORD; may I never forget the good things
he does for me. He forgives all my sins and heals all my diseases.
PSALM 103:2–3 NLT

Dear Lord, You have given Your only Son to die for me. Because of You and Your great gift, I have eternal life. You have forgiven my sins and healed my soul. Nothing is impossible with You in my life. Thank You for taking care of me. With all that I am, with my entire being, I praise You forever and ever!

....

....

....

....

Morning

SPIRIT-FILLED

*I have filled him with the Spirit of God, giving him great
wisdom, ability, and expertise in all kinds of crafts.*

Exodus 31:3 nlt

You have filled me with Your Spirit. I have been given wisdom, understanding, education, and talent for many lines of work. Show me how I can use my knowledge, understanding, and abilities to do the work You have set out for me. Show me the paths You want me to take. What do You want me to do with my hands, my life, my gifts? They all come from You, the One I want to serve.

....

....

....

....

....

Evening

GOD'S INSTRUCTIONS

*God said unto them, Be fruitful, and multiply, and replenish the earth,
and subdue it: and have dominion over the fish of the sea, and over the
fowl of the air, and over every living thing that moveth upon the earth.*

Genesis 1:28 kjv

From the earliest days of creation, You have been specific about what You want us to do, Lord. You said You want me to care for the earth in a way that pleases You. I want to learn what I can about Your creation so that I can appreciate it in all its splendor.

....

....

....

....

Morning
FEAR AND JOY

*"Surely God is my salvation; I will trust and not be afraid. The Lord,
the Lord, is my strength and my song; he has become my salvation."*
ISAIAH 12:2 NIV

Lord, fear is ugly and joy is beautiful. When fear is vanquished, joy becomes even more beautiful. So many people have a beautiful smile as they decide to follow You. They have replaced fear with the knowledge that they are following the One who sets aside all fear. I pray I will extinguish fear by remembering that I can put my trust in You.

....

....

....

....

....

Evening
BELIEF

"And whatever you ask in prayer, believing, you will receive it all."
MATTHEW 21:22 NASB

Without faith, I receive nothing from You, Lord. At times, my faith seems so small, all I can do is ask for Your help to believe. Even when the world seems to smash me down and my belief is small, I reach to You for help. As Your Spirit touches my heart again and I believe, I've already received the best: Your touch of new life for my spirit. I have so little to offer You, but I am trusting You today.

....

....

....

....

Morning
A TESTIMONY

And he hath put a new song in my mouth, even praise unto our
God: many shall see it, and fear, and shall trust in the LORD.
PSALM 40:3 KJV

My life is a song of praise to You, my faithful Father, the giver of life! When people hear my testimony of Your goodness, may they come to know You. I want others to notice the difference in me and wonder why I have such joy, such peace. May I point them to You, Lord, and may they trust in You for salvation. You are the way, the truth, and the life. Amen.

....

....

....

....

....

Evening
FOR THOSE IN PRISON

"I was in prison and you came to visit me."
MATTHEW 25:36 NIV

Lord, I pray for the men and women in prison all over our country today. I ask for a revival—that many would come to know You, love You, and serve You. Help those who are incarcerated know that You offer a life of hope and peace. In the darkness, help them find Christ's forgiveness, joy, and light. Remind my heart, Lord, to visit those in prison and fulfill Your commands.

....

....

....

....

....

Morning

MORNING MEDITATION

Give heed to the voice of my cry, my King and my God, for
to you I will pray. My voice You shall hear in the morning,
O LORD; in the morning I will direct it to You.

PSALM 5:2–3 NKJV

You defend me, You love me, You lead me. How great is that? You are too wonderful for words. This morning in Your presence, I rejoice. This morning, I direct my prayers to You, knowing that You will hear my words and interpret my groans. I am directing my voice to You, Lord, and patiently await Your instructions.

....

....

....

....

....

Evening

MUSIC

Whatsoever ye do, do all to the glory of God.

I CORINTHIANS 10:31 KJV

Dear Lord, music is the universal language of the human family. I want to base my choices on Your principles. What I listen to will affect my mood, my attitude, and my spiritual state of being. Holy Spirit, give me discernment. Let the music to which I listen not go counter to what You're trying to do in me. Amen.

....

....

....

....

Morning
QUIET WATERS

He makes me lie down in green pastures, he leads me beside quiet waters.
PSALM 23:2 NIV

My Shepherd, lead me beside the still waters. Lie with me in the green pastures. Restore my soul. Lead me down the paths of *Your* choosing today. With You by my side, I fear no evil. You are my Comfort and my Guide. I am happy in Your presence. Your goodness and Your mercy are with me this minute, this hour, and this day. Thank You, Lord, for leading me here and making me whole—for being the Shepherd of my life.

....

....

....

....

....

Evening
BLANK STARES

In all thy ways acknowledge him, and he shall direct thy paths.
PROVERBS 3:6 KJV

Today I'm struggling, Jesus. I have a specific goal that needs to be met, but it requires clarity of mind. The project is spread out before me, but I'm staring at it blankly. I know You want me to work on it, and I need Your guidance. Give me the ability to think and complete the task. Amen.

....

....

....

....

....

....

DAY 349

Morning
THE FIRST PRIORITY

"'Love the Lord your God with all your heart and with all your soul and with all your mind.' This is the first and greatest commandment."
MATTHEW 22:37–38 NIV

Father, You are my everything! Without You, I wouldn't even be here. Forgive me for allowing so many other things to squeeze between me and You. Help me become more diligent in my time with You. It fills me with the strength I need to make it day after day. I love You so much! I never want to take our relationship for granted.

....

....

....

....

....

Evening
SPECIAL INSTRUCTIONS

Thy word is a lamp unto my feet, and a light unto my path.
PSALM 119:105 KJV

Thank You for Your Word, Father. Without it I would be a hopeless case in regard to developing godly character. I'm so glad You preserved these special words that give me specific instruction on how to live. Help me hide these scriptures in my heart so that I'm able to rely on them throughout my life. Amen.

....

....

....

....

....

Morning
GOD'S GLORY, NOT MINE

Whatever you do, do all things for the glory of God.
1 CORINTHIANS 10:31 NASB

Everything I do today is for You, Lord. I refuse to get caught up in the mad rush. I refuse to seek only temporal satisfaction. I am here to please only You. Help me avoid stretching myself so thin that I am unable to do the things You ask. I am here for You and for You alone. Give me the energy I need to accomplish those tasks for Your glory. And tonight may You say, *"Ah, my good and faithful servant, well done!"*

....

....

....

....

....

Evening
BURDENS LIFTED

"Come to Me, all you who labor and are heavy laden, and I will give you rest."
MATTHEW 11:28 NKJV

Burdened—I know the feeling, Lord. You, the burden lifter, are not limited. Your Word promises You can hoist this weight from me and give me rest. I desperately need the rest You offer. The more I struggle for release, the more my burden weighs me down. Take all my sins and doubts, Lord, and exchange them for Your peace. Fill my heart with trust in my burden bearer.

....

....

....

....

....

Morning
WITH HIM EACH MOMENT

Seek first God's kingdom and what God wants.
Then all your other needs will be met as well.
MATTHEW 6:33 NCV

I can't seem to find any time, Lord. It's always rush, rush, rush. I need to remember that I am already with You in the heavens. Calm my heart. Help me breathe slower. I want to relax here at Your feet. I want to smell Your perfume, touch Your robe, hear Your voice. When I do Your work today, everything else will then fall into place. I lean back against Your knees, waiting to hear Your voice.

....

....

....

....

Evening
A BLESSING OF PEACE

"The LORD bless you and keep you; the LORD make his face shine on you and
be gracious to you; the LORD turn his face toward you and give you peace."
NUMBERS 6:24–26 NIV

Lord, long ago You told Moses to have Aaron and his sons bless the Israelites with these words. I ask that You would bless me with peace as I pray this prayer. Let Your love and mercy shine on me so I can be a light that shines the way for others.

....

....

....

....

....

Morning

RELENTLESS PRAYING

[Daniel] continued kneeling on his knees three times a day, praying and offering praise before his God, just as he had been doing previously.

DANIEL 6:10 NASB

"As he had been doing previously"—what amazing words! Help me be like Daniel, Lord. When faced with arrest and execution, when all seemed bleak and hopeless, he didn't panic but did as he had always done. He came before You on his knees, offering praise. Keep me close to You, Lord. Enter my heart as I kneel at Your throne.

....

....

....

....

....

Evening

THINGS NOT SEEN

Now faith is the substance of things hoped for, the evidence of things not seen.

HEBREWS 11:1 KJV

Jesus, it is easy to believe in that which I can see. I wish I could reach out and touch You. As I meditate on Your Word, give me faith in that which I cannot see. Give me faith that all of Your promises are true and that one day You will come again in the clouds to take me home. Amen.

....

....

....

....

....

....

Morning

ONE-TOUCH HEALING

For she said to herself, "If only I may touch His garment, I shall be made well."
MATTHEW 9:21 NKJV

Dear God, I am reaching out my hand to You this morning, knowing that if I can just touch the hem of Your garment, You will make me whole. I envision You before me. I see the compassion in Your eyes. I know that You love me and that nothing is impossible for You. Fill me with Your love. Give me Your healing touch this morning.

....

....

....

....

....

Evening

MAKE LOVE YOUR AIM

The goal of this command is love, which comes from a pure heart and a good conscience and a sincere faith.
1 TIMOTHY 1:5 NIV

Lord, may my highest aim be love. Love is Your greatest commandment. Fill me with Your unconditional and accepting love and empower me to care deeply and well for others. May the love I give come from a pure heart, uncontaminated by selfishness. Help me have the right motives and be genuinely and sincerely concerned about other people's lives.

....

....

....

....

....

Morning

KEEPING PRIORITIES STRAIGHT

"God is with you in all that you do."

GENESIS 21:22 NKJV

Lord, as I go through this day, help me keep my priorities straight. It's not all about what I do but how I treat others. Show me how to love those I come in contact with as I go through my daily routine and run my errands. Help me be a person of compassion. When people see me, I want them to recognize You, because that's what the world needs more of these days—Your love, Your face, Your presence, Your light.

....

....

....

....

....

Evening

GOD IS FAITHFUL

But the Lord is faithful, who shall stablish you, and keep you from evil.

2 THESSALONIANS 3:3 KJV

God, I focus a lot on my faith in You. And then You show me that it is not all about me. You are faithful to me. You show me how to be faithful. You never leave. You never give up on me. You never turn away. You always show up. You always believe in me. You are faithful by Your very nature. You cannot be unfaithful. Thank You for Your faithfulness in my life. Amen.

....

....

....

....

....

Morning
BEARING FRUIT

He shall be like a tree planted by the rivers of water, that brings forth its fruit in its season, whose leaf also shall not wither; and whatever he does shall prosper.

PSALM 1:3 NKJV

I come to You this morning, meditating on Your Word. That is my living water. You are the quencher of my thirst; You provide everything for me. As I go through the activities of this day, may Your hand be upon me. To Your good and great glory, Lord, amen!

Evening
CONTENTED!

The fear of the LORD leads to life, and he who has it will abide in satisfaction; he will not be visited with evil.

PROVERBS 19:23 NKJV

You are powerful beyond anything our hearts and minds can imagine. I need not go in fear of You, though. You have made me Your child, and that makes all the difference. You've offered me rest in You, and I've accepted. You no longer want my fear but my faith. In You, my heart need never dread. I'm trusting in my Lord and rest content.

Morning
MY MAIN DESIRE

One thing I have desired of the LORD, that will I seek: that I may
dwell in the house of the LORD all the days of my life, to behold
the beauty of the LORD, and to inquire in His temple.

PSALM 27:4 NKJV

Lord, help me keep the main thing the main thing—and that is to seek
first the kingdom of God, beholding Your beauty, inquiring in Your temple.
That is all that is truly important. As I receive requests for my time, give
me wisdom to answer in accordance with Your will.

....

....

....

....

Evening
BEING GODLY ON PURPOSE

And be not conformed to this world: but be ye transformed
by the renewing of your mind, that ye may prove what is
that good, and acceptable, and perfect, will of God.

ROMANS 12:2 KJV

Lord, I was recently reminded that godly character doesn't just happen. I
have to purpose in my heart to live a life pleasing to You. Only then will I
be able to stand strong when peer pressure threatens to undo me. I want
to commit daily to obeying You. Amen.

....

....

....

....

....

Morning
BUSY DAYS

Anxiety in the heart of man causes depression, but a good word makes it glad.
PROVERBS 12:25 NKJV

Here I am, Lord, getting ready for another busy day. Help me stay calm and not get caught up in the frenzied pace. Sure and steady wins the race, and my race is to win the prize of Your presence in my life. Help me keep that in the forefront of my mind today. May I not become anxious but keep Your Word of peace in my heart and be a beacon of peace in the presence of others.

....

....

....

....

....

Evening
RESTING ON THE SABBATH

Remember the sabbath day, to keep it holy. Six days shalt thou labour, and do all thy work: but the seventh day is the sabbath of the LORD thy God: in it thou shalt not do any work.
EXODUS 20:8–10 KJV

Father, You created us as beings who work and need rest. Sometimes I forget that. I get so caught up in all that must be accomplished. Slow my pace, Lord. Help me honor You by resting one day per week. Help me keep the Sabbath holy. Thank You for designing the week and for telling Your people to rest. It is up to me to follow Your command. Amen.

....

....

....

....

Morning
I WILL FOLLOW YOU

Then he said to them all: "Whoever wants to be my disciple must deny themselves and take up their cross daily and follow me. For whoever wants to save their life will lose it, but whoever loses their life for me will save it."

LUKE 9:23–24 NIV

Lord, I am ready to "take up my cross" and follow You. Every day I want to be empowered by You. Show me what it means to lose my life in order to save it. Teach me about surrender; I know You lift me up to do Your good purposes. Transform me, Lord.

....

....

....

....

....

Evening
SAVED BY GRACE THROUGH FAITH

For by grace are ye saved through faith; and that not of yourselves: it is the gift of God: not of works, lest any man should boast.

EPHESIANS 2:8–9 KJV

God, it is so comforting to know that my position before You is secure. When You look at me, because I have been saved through faith, You see Your Son in me. You no longer see sin but righteousness. I couldn't have earned it, no matter how hard I worked. Thank You for the gift of salvation through my faith in Jesus. Amen.

....

....

....

....

Morning

LET'S GROW

Like newborn babies, crave pure spiritual milk,
so that by it you may grow up in your salvation.
1 PETER 2:2 NIV

Lord, I want to grow up spiritually. I want to transition from a newborn baby who drinks only milk to a more mature believer who craves the "meat" of deeper things. I want to move from head knowledge to heart experience with You. I want to know what it means to enjoy Your presence, not just to make requests. Step by step and day by day, teach me to follow and learn Your ways.

....

....

....

....

....

Evening

THE CENTER OF GOD'S WILL

Commit thy works unto the LORD, and thy thoughts shall be established.
PROVERBS 16:3 KJV

Lord, I know that in the center of Your will are peace, joy, and many other rich blessings. I'd like to experience all these things, but the trouble I seem to have is figuring out what Your will is for me. Please help me be attentive when You speak, and give me a heart willing to be used by You. Amen.

....

....

....

....

....

Morning
GOD'S PRESENCE

"The virgin will conceive and give birth to a son, and they will call him Immanuel" (which means, "God with us").

MATTHEW 1:23 NIV

Lord, thank You for sending Your Son, "God with Us," Emmanuel. Born of a virgin, You came to point us to the truth that saves us. You chose twelve disciples who followed You and learned the way to really live. You healed the sick; You gave sight to the blind. You were known for Your miracles and radical love for all kinds of people. Thank You for Your presence and that You live in me today.

....

....

....

....

Evening
REST IN GOD

The LORD replied, "My Presence will go with you, and I will give you rest."

EXODUS 33:14 NIV

Challenging circumstances don't disturb me much when I'm at peace in You. I may not be great or famous, but You still ask me to draw near and feel the calm You give. As Your child, I am asked to draw ever closer to You, day by day. Today I need Your presence, Lord. Help me rest in You always. Like Moses, I'm nothing on my own.

....

....

....

....

....

Morning

RESTORED RELATIONSHIPS

*We, too, have put our faith in Christ Jesus that we may be
justified by faith in Christ and not by the works of the law,
because by the works of the law no one will be justified.*

GALATIANS 2:16 NIV

Lord, You know how painful it is when things are not right between friends.
I long for connected relationships, where people live in peace and harmony.
What a joy it is to know that I am made right with God by faith. I want
to live in a growing love relationship with You. Thank You for restoration
and righteousness.

....

....

....

....

Evening

GRANTING FORGIVENESS

*"And whenever you stand praying, if you have anything against anyone,
forgive him, that your Father in heaven may also forgive you your trespasses."*

MARK 11:25 NKJV

Heavenly Father, I need to forgive someone who wronged me. I know it's
the right thing, but it's so difficult. I can't do it in my own strength. Give me
the power to extend grace to this person. Put Your love in my heart so I can
have a gracious attitude and a heart of mercy. I'm leaning on Your power. In
Jesus' name, amen.

....

....

....

....

....

Morning

GIFT OF THE HOLY SPIRIT

"You have made known to me the paths of life;
you will fill me with joy in your presence."
ACTS 2:28 NIV

Lord, I have repented of my sins and asked You to come into my life. I have received Your forgiveness. I thank You that Your Holy Spirit now lives inside me. What a gift! I choose to acknowledge this gift and ask that You would empower me to live a Spirit-filled life. Let my thoughts and actions be full of life and light and love, so others may see Christ in me.

....

....

....

....

Evening

CHRIST'S LONELINESS

Fear thou not; for I am with thee: be not dismayed; for I am
thy God: I will strengthen thee; yea, I will help thee; yea, I
will uphold thee with the right hand of my righteousness.
ISAIAH 41:10 KJV

Lord, how alone You must have been in the garden when the disciples fell asleep. And when God turned His back as You hung on the cross—was there anything to compare to what You felt? Yet You did it willingly. You understand when I'm lonely, and I thank You for being there during those times. Amen.

....

....

....

....

....

Morning

POWER OF THE CROSS

For the message of the cross is foolishness to those who are perishing,
but to us who are being saved it is the power of God.

1 CORINTHIANS 1:18 NIV

Lord, I thank You for the wisdom to know the truth. Your power is amazing; there is no one like You. No one else can bring the dead back to life, perform miracles, and change lives like mine. Please help other people know the power of the cross too.

....

....

....

....

....

Evening

POWER BOOST

He gives power to the weak, and to those who have no might He
increases strength. . . . Those who wait on the LORD shall renew
their strength; they shall mount up with wings like eagles, they
shall run and not be weary, they shall walk and not faint.

ISAIAH 40:29, 31 NKJV

Dear God, I'm stuck in a cycle of busyness that has no end in sight. There are constant demands on my energy and sanity. I feel like I go through life in a state of exhaustion. I know that keeps me from being at my peak. Show me what I can change, Lord.

....

....

....

....

Morning
PRAYER FOR SALVATION

*If you declare with your mouth, "Jesus is Lord," and believe in
your heart that God raised him from the dead, you will be saved.*

ROMANS 10:9 NIV

Lord, I humbly bow before you now and confess my sins to you. I ask Your
forgiveness. I believe Jesus is the Son of God, and that He died on a cross
and was raised from the dead. He conquered death so that I might really
live—in power and purpose here on earth and forever with Him in heaven.
I choose You. Please be my Savior and my Lord.

....

....

....

....

....

Evening
TEARS

Put my tears into Your bottle; are they not in Your book?

PSALM 56:8 NKJV

I've heard, God, that tears speak their own language. Like most women, I
cry for a variety of reasons, and sometimes for no reason at all, like today.
But since You read what's in my heart, I know You understand. Thank You
for valuing my tears. Amen.

....

....

....

....

....

....

Morning
STRONG ARMS

"The eternal God is your refuge, and underneath are the everlasting arms.
He will drive out your enemies before you, saying, 'Destroy them!'"
DEUTERONOMY 33:27 NIV

Your strong, everlasting arms hold me safely, Lord, even in trouble. Help me believe You are always there for me, forever keeping me from harm. I want to live and trust in You, instead of falling into danger because I doubt Your care. Hold me tight today, Lord Jesus. I need Your protection from every enemy—spiritual and temporal—that comes against me. You are my only refuge, Lord.

....

....

....

....

....

Evening
THANK YOU FOR SAVING ME

Thanks be to God for his indescribable gift!
2 CORINTHIANS 9:15 NIV

Lord, I thank You for my salvation. I thank You for Your indescribable gift of eternal life and the power to do Your will today. I can hardly fathom how You suffered, yet You did it all for me—for every person on this planet. Mocked and beaten, You bled for my sins. You had victory over death so we could live. You made a way for me, and I am eternally grateful. Thank You, Lord.

....

....

....

....

Scripture Index

Journal Your Journey of Faith

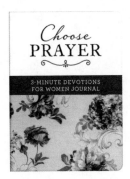

Choose Prayer: 3-Minute Devotions for Women Journal

Written especially for women like you, this devotional journal packs a powerful dose of comfort, encouragement, and reflection into just-right-sized readings. Each day's reading is complemented by a relevant scripture and prayer.

Flexible Casebound / 978-1-64352-625-6 / $12.99

Cultivating Confidence: A Faith-Building Devotional Journal

Featuring two hundred devotional readings complemented by scripture selections and prayers, this lovely journal offers a powerful blend of inspiration, encouragement, and assurance for every area of your life.

Flexible Casebound / 978-1-63609-195-2 / $12.99